JOSSEY-BASS TEACHER

Jossey-Bass Teacher provides K–12 teachers with essential knowledge and tools to create a positive and lifelong impact on student learning. Trusted and experienced educational mentors offer practical classroom-tested and theory-based teaching resources for improving teaching practice in a broad range of grade levels and subject areas. From one educator to another, we want to be your first source to make every day your best day in teaching. *Jossey-Bass Teacher* resources serve two types of informational needs: essential knowledge and essential tools.

Essential knowledge resources provide the foundation, strategies, and methods from which teachers may design curriculum and instruction to challenge and excite their students. Connecting theory to practice, essential knowledge books rely on a solid research base and time-tested methods, offering the best ideas and guidance from many of the most experienced and well-respected experts in the field. Essential tools save teachers time and effort by offering proven, ready-to-use materials for in-class use. Our publications include activities, assessments, exercises, instruments, games, ready reference, and more. They enhance an entire course of study, a weekly lesson, or a daily plan. These essential tools provide insightful, practical, and comprehensive materials on topics that matter most to K–12 teachers.

MC REL

Mid-Continent Research in Education and Learning (McREL) is an internation-
ally recognized private, nonprofit organization located in Aurora, Colorado, ded-
icated to improving education for all students through applied research,
production development, and service. Its staff of highly respected educators and
researchers focuses on providing educators and policymakers with the highest-
quality, field-tested, research-based products and services available in pre-K–16
education. McREL offers a wide array of workshops to schools, districts, and in-
termediate service agencies across the country. Contact us at 303-337-0990 or
info@mcrel.org to learn how McREL experts can help your school or district learn
from research how to improve student achievement.

For the Love of Words

For the Love of Words

VOCABULARY INSTRUCTION THAT WORKS, GRADES K–6

Diane E. Paynter
Elena Bodrova
Jane K. Doty

Foreword by
Nell K. Duke,
Ed.D.

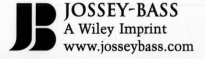

JOSSEY-BASS
A Wiley Imprint
www.josseybass.com

Published by Jossey-Bass
A Wiley Imprint
989 Market Street, San Francisco, CA 94103-1741   www.josseybass.com

Jossey-Bass books and products are available through most bookstores. To contact Jossey-Bass directly, call our Customer Care Department within the U.S. at 800-956-7739, outside the U.S. at 317-572-3986, or fax 317-572-4002.

Jossey-Bass also publishes its books in a variety of electronic formats. Some content that appears in print may not be available in electronic books.

Library of Congress Cataloging-in-Publication Data

Paynter, Diane E.
  For the love of words : vocabulary instruction that works, grades K-6 / Diane E. Paynter, Elena Bodrova, Jane K. Doty ; foreword by Nell K. Duke.— 1st ed.
     p. cm. — (Jossey-Bass teacher)
  Includes bibliographical references and index.
  ISBN-13 978-0-7879-7784-9
  ISBN-10 0-7879-7784-5 (alk. paper)
  1. Vocabulary—Study and teaching (Elementary)—United States. I. Bodrova, Elena. II. Doty, Jane K. III. Title. IV. Series.
  LB1574.5.P39 2005
  372.61—dc22

                          2005009300

Printed in the United States of America
FIRST EDITION
PB Printing   10 9 8 7 6 5 4 3 2

CONTENTS

To my family—George, Jen, Brooke, and Ben.
There are not enough words to describe my love for you.

—Diane Paynter

To my first teachers, my parents—David and Suzanne.
Thank you for teaching me the love, the power, and the significance of words.

—Jane Doty

With love to my family—Dmitri and Andrei Semenov.

—Elena Bodrova

Kudos to you for holding this book in your hands! It is so easy to neglect vocabulary. For years the topic has been rated "not hot" in the International Reading Association's annual survey of literacy topics, although, happily, this has recently changed. The topic too often does not make the list of those slated for district or state professional development, and many instructional programs include little, or misguided, attention to vocabulary. Moreover, as the authors of this book point out, we receive many discouraging messages about vocabulary—for example, that children enter school with incredibly large gaps in their vocabularies or that they need to learn more words than we can possibly teach. Given messages like this, it is hard to feel we can make a difference, and so it is tempting to place vocabulary low on our priority list.

Many factors have made it easy to neglect vocabulary, but this book makes it much easier *not* to. The book offers practical, informed advice about providing an effective vocabulary program in elementary classrooms. It deals with those sticky issues that plague us: How do we decide which words to teach? How do we assess children's knowledge of these words? How does independent reading or the ever-elusive incidental learning fit in? What techniques are better suited for younger students, older students, and English Language Learners? What role is there for dictionaries, thesauruses, electronic resources, and many others?

But of all the topics on which to spend your valuable reading and professional development time, why vocabulary? In Chapter One, the authors offer many reasons—for example, that differences in people's vocabulary are related to differences in school success, ability to learn new things, writing effectiveness, even income. I want to draw attention to one of these reasons: that vocabulary enables reading comprehension (Baumann, Kame'enui, and Ash, 2003; Blachowicz and Fisher, 2000; National Reading Panel, 2000; Stahl, 1998; Stahl and Fairbanks, 1986). Students with larger vocabularies tend to have measurably higher reading comprehension, and students with limited vocabularies are impeded in their ability to comprehend. As educators, we regularly see situations in which even relatively strong students cannot understand what they are reading because they simply do not know enough of the necessary vocabulary. Yet research does indeed suggest that teaching vocabulary improves reading comprehension. For many teachers, increasing students' comprehension is their number one goal; intense vocabulary building is a tool for meeting this goal.

Intermingled, intertwined, inextricable, entangled, engaged, enmeshed: these are some of my vocabulary words for explaining the relationship between reading comprehension and vocabulary. Vocabulary builds reading comprehension, and the converse is true as well: reading comprehension builds vocabulary (Nagy, Herman, and Anderson, 1987). This more often overlooked truism is well reflected throughout this book. The authors explain that a portion of the vocabulary we learn each year comes directly from reading. They note that this is especially true as children move into the upper elementary grades, but it can also be true, particularly through read-alouds, for children in the primary grades. The authors also underscore the need for multiple exposures to a word for word learning, with reading an important source of second and tertiary exposures to words, even if they are first introduced through conversation or instruction. The role that understanding prefixes, suffixes, and roots can play in vocabulary development is also emphasized in this book. In some cases—for example, with the words *sign* and *signal* or *sane* and *sanity*—these relationships can be detected only when words are seen in written form (Venezky, 1999). Finally, the authors make it clear that books and other written texts are a major resource for identifying words to be the focus of vocabulary instruction. As they rightly point out, most new words we want children to learn after early childhood are more often found in written texts than in everyday conversations. Thus, the process they describe in Chapter Six for identifying words for instruction includes text in several ways.

For all these reasons, as a researcher and educator primarily concerned with improving children's reading comprehension, I implore you to read this book on vocabulary. Your time will be well spent. As the authors aptly explain in the Preface, there are many characteristics that make the book unique and that will very well serve the classroom teacher or reading specialist interested in a comprehensive approach to vocabulary building in elementary school. The authors have done an important service to the field in this book, and you will do an important service to the field in implementing the strategies within. Sincere thanks to all of you.

Nell K. Duke, Ed.D.
Michigan State University

As you open this book, you are probably wondering: Why another book on teaching vocabulary? Aren't there enough books that address this topic already? How will this book be different?

For many years, we have been fascinated by the research on the effects of a limited vocabulary on student achievement. Specifically, in the past five years, we have worked closely with those elementary and secondary schools listed in the acknowledgments of this book in the application of this research. It is these interactions that prompted us to write this book.

When we began working on this book, we were asking ourselves the same questions. The answers came from our experiences as researchers and teacher trainers; we are in classrooms watching and listening to teachers. What we hear again and again is that the task of teaching vocabulary to elementary students is overwhelming and overshadowed by the task of teaching more basic reading skills. We also hear that many of the teaching strategies found in other books are too generic and do not address the learning characteristics of younger learners or prepare upper elementary students for the challenges of understanding the vocabulary in middle and high school texts. Many teachers have concerns about the vocabulary programs they are using because they focus on words that students are already familiar with or on words that are not meaningful to the content students need to be learning.

As we worked to address these concerns, we developed a concern of our own: the urgency of closing the gap in vocabulary learning between students who arrive at school with a rich vocabulary and those who arrive with a poor vocabulary. Our solution for addressing many of these concerns was to include a chapter about the developmental aspects of learning vocabulary.

We reviewed different approaches to teaching vocabulary and concluded that not all words students learn need to be taught in a systematic fashion, and of these, only a portion require direct instruction. We have also tried to address the somewhat confusing notion of "incidental" vocabulary learning (can we really leave such important learning to chance?) and provide teachers with suggestions for how they can plan for such learning to occur. Finally, we focused on different ways to assess student vocabulary learning that teachers can use to fine-tune their classroom instruction. Although we have tried to make this book as practical as possible, we want it to be viewed not as a collection of useful activities but rather as a framework for planning all aspects of systematic vocabulary instruction.

In short, *For the Love of Words: Vocabulary Instruction That Works* will help you:

- Realize the importance of teaching vocabulary and the connection between a student's rich vocabulary and success in school (Chapter One)

- Understand the current research on the developmental differences in how children learn vocabulary from kindergarten through grade 6 (Chapter Two)

- Understand a variety of approaches to teaching vocabulary (Chapter Three)

- Learn a process and strategies that can be used for direct instruction (Chapter Four)

- Learn ways to teach new words through planned incidental learning experiences (Chapter Five)

- Create a customized list of vocabulary terms and phrases that aligns with the content you teach and builds a strong foundation for general literacy (Chapter Six)

- Determine how and when students will learn the vocabulary words from your list (Chapter Seven)

- Collect evidence on students' progress in learning new vocabulary (Chapter Eight)

- Devise a system for keeping records of the words students are learning (Chapter Eight)

- Use the list of basic words by Robert J. Marzano, John S. Kendall, and Diane E. Paynter as a tool for creating the customized list of vocabulary terms and phrases for your grade level (Appendix).

We hope that as you read the chapters in this book, our enthusiasm for setting up a systematic approach to vocabulary learning will be contagious and that the framework we present will provide you the support needed to make improvements in the way you teach vocabulary in your classroom.

ACKNOWLEDGMENTS

We thank the Indiana State Department of Education, which made it possible for us to work with the following mentors, districts, and schools in Indiana in the development and refinement of the practices and strategies found in this book:

Indiana Department of Education

Ilene G. Block

Alice Harpel

Elizabeth Skeen

Teacher Mentors

Jolinda Bove	Cindy Hurst	Sandi Stanfield
Brenda Bridge	Anita Kishel	Ruth Swetnam
Shirley Byrer	Amy Leeson	Cheryl Thomas
Tala Clay	Marti Mauntel	Judy Weber
Linda Cornwell	Jamie Miller	Claudia Wheatley
Mida Creekmur	Kathleen Schneider	
Rhonda Hays	Jerry Slauter	

Indiana School Districts

Cannelton City Schools

Knox Community School Corporation

Indiana School Districts (continued)

Medora Community School Corporation

MSD Shakamak Schools

North White School Corporation

River Forest Community School Corporation

Switzerland County School Corporation

Indiana Schools

Allen Elementary School

Break-O-Day Elementary

Brunswick Elementary School

Caldwell Elementary School

Center Elementary School

Columbia Elementary School

Drew Elementary School

Eastern Pulaski Elementary

Ernie Pyle Elementary School

Frances Slocum Elementary School

Garden City Elementary School

Hamilton Elementary School

Henry W. Eggers Middle School

Huntingburg Elementary School

Kuny Elementary School

Lafayette Elementary School

Lincoln Elementary

Maywood Elementary School

North Judson San Pierre Elementary

School City of Hammond

Southeast Elementary School

Wes-Del Elementary School

In addition, we thank the following individuals who were instrumental in giving us valuable feedback and support in writing this book:

Suzanne Loughran, principal, Cottonwood Elementary School, Cherry Creek Schools, Englewood, Colorado

Richard Sjolseth and Diane Watanabe, Los Angeles County Office of Education's Institute of Learning, Teaching and the Human Brain, Los Angeles, California

Deena Tarleton, principal, Vienna International School, Vienna, Austria

We especially thank two members of the McREL staff who made this book possible: Adrienne Schure, senior director of product development, and Brian Lancaster, graphic designer.

THE AUTHORS

Diane E. Paynter is a senior director in field services at Mid-Continent Research for Education and Learning in Aurora, Colorado. An international trainer and researcher, she has worked extensively at the state, district, building, and classroom levels in the areas of standards, curriculum and instruction, assessment, grading and record keeping, vocabulary, and literacy development. As director of consortia, Paynter works with various consortia across the United States, providing direction, training, materials, and technical support as they move toward aligning curriculum, instruction, record keeping and reporting, and assessment practices to standards. Paynter has authored many books, instructional units, and articles.

Elena Bodrova is a senior researcher at Mid-Continent Research for Education and Learning (McREL) in Aurora, Colorado, and a research fellow at the National Institute for Early Education Research. Prior to joining McREL, Bodrova was a visiting professor of educational psychology at the Metropolitan State College of Denver, senior researcher at the Russian Center for Educational Innovations, senior researcher at the Russian Institute for Preschool Education, and adjunct professor of educational psychology at Moscow Teacher Training College. She holds an M.A. in developmental and educational psychology from Moscow State University and a Ph.D. in developmental and educational psychology from the Russian Academy of Pedagogical Sciences. She is the author of numerous articles and book chapters on early literacy, play, and assessment.

Jane K. Doty, an international trainer and author, is a principal consultant for Mid-Continent Research for Education and Learning in Aurora, Colorado, and has nearly twenty years of experience as an educator. She consults with school districts to assist them in the process of aligning standards and benchmarks, developing curriculum units, and training educators in *Dimensions of Learning,* effective classroom instruction, and *Teaching Reading in the Content Areas.* She is coauthor of *Teaching Reading in Social Studies.* She has also worked on educational projects with Disney, ABC, and PBS. She recently received a commendation from the governor of Indiana for her work with educators in the Indiana TOPHAT Consortia. Doty earned her certificate of advanced study in educational administration from the State University of New York at Oswego, an M.S. in gifted education from the State University of New York at Plattsburgh, and a B.S. in elementary education from Keuka College.

For the Love of Words

The Importance of Developing a Robust Vocabulary

The limits of my language are the limits of my mind.
All I know is what I have words for.

Ludwig Wittgenstein

Four-year-old Ben finds a treat in the bottom of a box of cereal. "What is it?" he asks, and Mom replies, "It's an animal that lived long ago. It's called a dinosaur." Satisfied with her explanation, Ben runs off to play with his new toy. Several days later, he sees his dinosaur on television and points this out to Dad. Dad explains that his dinosaur is a *Tyrannosaurus rex* and then proceeds to give Ben labels for the other kinds of dinosaurs they see on television. Ben repeats the names. He likes how grown-up the words sound and the way they roll around in his mouth. As he watches the dinosaurs, he tells his dad what he sees: "That dinosaur flies like a bird. That one walks like a dog." He is making connections about dinosaurs to what he already knows.

A few weeks later, Grandma comes to visit. Since Ben's enthusiasm for dinosaurs has spilled over into their weekly telephone conversations, she brings Ben a book about dinosaurs, and together they look at the pictures as she reads the book aloud to him. Over time, Ben discovers that dinosaurs lived long, long ago and now are extinct. He also learns that some dinosaurs were very mean and even ate other animals, and now he has words like *flesh-eating* and *carnivore* to describe this. On the next trip to the library, Ben looks for more books about dinosaurs, as he seems to have an unquenchable thirst to learn all he can about these formidable animals.

One day Ben decides to bring his collection of dinosaurs to kindergarten for sharing time. As he prepares to present them to the class, his teacher asks the students what they know about dinosaurs. Rachel says dinosaurs lived long ago. The teacher acknowledges Rachel's comment and says, "Yes, that's right, Rachel. Now they are extinct. An animal or plant becomes extinct when there are no more of its kind alive." Jamal adds that some dinosaurs were bigger than a bus. His teacher agrees and elaborates, "That's right. Some of the dinosaurs were enormous." Then Ben shares some of what he knows about dinosaurs, which could be represented on a diagram like the one in Figure 1.1.

This word web is one way to show how new words relate to known words. Ben already knows some things about animals and uses what he knows about them to construct meaning for the word *dinosaur.* Some of the new words, such as *immense, gigantic,* and *skeleton,* are useful in other settings. Ben made this clear when he explained that at the museum, he saw "the skeleton of a Brontosaurus that was as immense as the new hotel they were building near the gas station."

Because of Ben's interest in dinosaurs, he receives several toy dinosaurs for his birthday. His dad tells him the names of his new toys: Pteranodon, Allosaurus, and Stegosaurus. He begins to make finer and finer distinctions among his dinosaurs and learns new names that relate to them. For example, he learns that a Stegosaurus has "platelets" on its back and the Pteranodon has "talons." Ben's fascination with dinosaurs, initially motivated by a new toy, results in his actively acquiring a network of words and concepts about them. He learns their names, and when he is sufficiently confident in his knowledge, he shares his dinosaur collection with

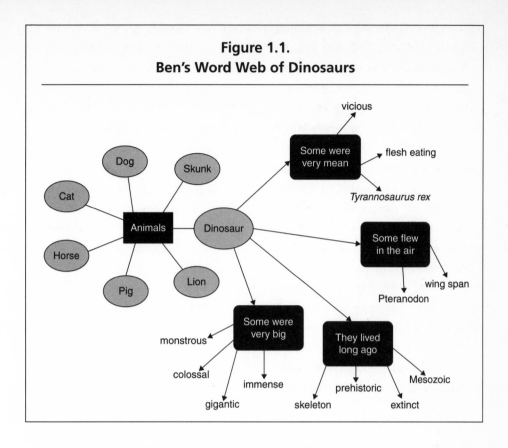

**Figure 1.1.
Ben's Word Web of Dinosaurs**

others. The admiring feedback he receives will probably motivate him to learn even more about dinosaurs. Who knows? A cereal box toy could inspire Ben to become a paleontologist.

VOCABULARY AND ACADEMIC SUCCESS

Ben is developing what Isabel Beck calls a "robust" vocabulary—one that is "vigorous, strong, and powerful" (Beck, McKeown, and Kucan, 2002). By the end of kindergarten, he already has many "tags" or "labels" stored in his long-term memory. As he encounters new experiences, images, and their accompanying tags, his vocabulary will continue to expand, and he will continue to use what he already knows to construct meaning for these new words. It is safe to say that every new *gigantic* thing Ben encounters will be compared to the gigantic-ness of dinosaurs. With his growing vo-cabulary, he will not only recognize more words in conversations, when he is being read to, and in written form as he develops his literacy skills; he will also have greater comprehension skills because he can bring meaning to these experiences. Ben is well on his way to success in school.

Like Ben, other children with robust vocabularies understand a great deal of what they hear, see, and read because they know a lot of words. The words children know represent the conceptual understanding they have, even if it is surface knowledge. This knowledge helps them construct meaning for new words and information they are receiving. Decades of research on learning conclude that "people construct new knowledge and understanding based on what they already know and believe" (Bransford, Brown, and Cocking, 2000, p. 10). In short, students' prior knowledge helps them learn new things more easily.

Hearing new labels for things allows students to see what they have not seen before—to clarify and enrich the meaning of concepts they may already be somewhat familiar with. From a very young age, they know what flowers are, and as they get older, they learn the words for specific flowers: *rose, tulip, lilac, daisy, buttercup.* These finer distinctions among words help them develop a deeper, more flexible understanding of the core meaning of words. Ultimately they come to understand how the same word can have different meanings. For example, in the primary grades, children start to appreciate jokes like, "Why is it cool at a baseball game?" The answer: "Because all the fans are there."

If their vocabulary is meager, they are limited in what they see and understand. Certainly Ben was able to see many distinctions before he learned his new vocabulary words, but the increasingly sophisticated labels he was learning allowed him to see beyond the visible and understand more abstract concepts, such as flesh eating versus plant eating. His vocabulary was becoming much more transferable and robust.

Learners with robust vocabularies are attuned to new words. They are word conscious, which means they are aware of, intrigued by, and interested in language. Word consciousness motivates their learning. Puns, idioms, and familiar words in unusual contexts, such as a *pod of whales* (Figure 1.2) or a *corned beef* (Figure 1.3), excite the imagination of students with rich, robust vocabularies. As their vocabularies expand, their capacity to make sense of the world around them and express themselves to others is heightened.

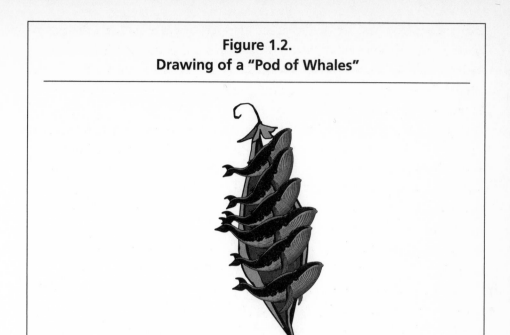

Figure 1.2.
Drawing of a "Pod of Whales"

Certainly a robust vocabulary is essential; we need words to develop our capacity to speak, read, and write. It is through vocabulary, oral and written, that we comprehend information and express ourselves. According to the 2000 Report of the National Reading Panel, *Teaching Children to Read,*

> Vocabulary occupies an important position in learning to read. As a learner begins to read, reading vocabulary encountered in texts is mapped onto the oral vocabulary the learner brings to the task. That is, the reader is taught to translate the (relatively) unfamiliar words in print into speech, with the expectation that the speech forms will be easier to comprehend. A benefit in understanding text by applying letter-sound correspondences to printed material only comes about if the resultant oral representation is a known word in the learner's oral vocabulary. If the resultant oral vocabulary is not in the learner's vocabulary, it will not be better understood than it was in print. Thus,

Figure 1.3.
Drawing of "Corned Beef"

vocabulary seems to occupy an important middle ground in learning to read. Oral vocabulary is a key to learning to make the transition from oral to written forms, whereas reading vocabulary is crucial to the comprehension process of a skilled reader [p. 4-15].

OVERCOMING THE VOCABULARY GAP

That Ben arrived at school with a robust vocabulary and an extensive network of words will have a tremendous effect on his success in school. But what will happen to those students who come to school with small vocabularies and little ability to make connections between the meanings of words? "One of the most consistent findings of educational research is that having a small vocabulary portends poor school performance and, conversely, that having a large vocabulary is associated with school success" (Anderson and Nagy, 1993, p. 6). Is there really that much of a vocabulary gap among students, and does this gap have that much of an effect on their success in school?

The answer to these questions is a resounding yes. The difference in the number of words students know as they enter school is startling and related to socioeconomic status (SES). In 1982, researchers found that in a domain of 5,044 words, first graders with low SES knew about 1,800 words. Their middle-class counterparts knew approximately 2,700 words (Graves, 1986; Graves, Brunetti, and Slater, 1982). Using a larger domain of over 19,000 words, the same researchers found that the disadvantaged first graders knew about 2,900 words compared to the middle-class students' 5,800 words. Students in middle-class schools learn about 5,200 new words a year. Students in lower-SES schools learn about 3,500 words a year (Baker, Simmons, and Kame'enui, 1995). It is clear that economically disadvantaged students have a dramatically smaller vocabulary than their middle-class counterparts.

The research on the effects of the so-called vocabulary gap is powerful (see Marzano, Pickering, and Pollock, 2001, for the review of research). In addition to the "well-documented link between vocabulary size and early reading ability" (Snow, Burns, and Griffin, 1998, p. 47), vocabulary size was found to be associated with the ability to comprehend new information (Chall, 1958; Harrison, 1980) and even with income level (Sticht, Hofstetter, and Hofstetter, 1997).

In other words, children who have poor vocabularies are at a great disadvantage in school and in the rest of life. It is more difficult for students with fewer concepts to construct meaning from what they hear or read because they have limited background knowledge. Consequently, the new words they encounter may have little meaning for them, making it difficult for them to remember and use these words. In contrast, students with larger vocabularies continue to build their vocabularies at rates that widen the gap between the two groups. And yet current research suggests that in many classrooms, not much attention is paid to vocabulary (Ryder and Graves, 1994; Watts, 1995).

Although this all sounds rather distressing, the good news is that if children with limited vocabulary are provided vocabulary-rich experiences in school, they too can learn new words. In other words, a lack of vocabulary in students is not genetically based; rather, it is based on lack of meaningful experiences with words. So if children have not developed their vocabularies by the age of three, the window of opportunity does not close. It is never too late to begin building a robust vocabulary.

PLANNING VOCABULARY INSTRUCTION IN YOUR CLASSROOM

As a classroom teacher, you undoubtedly see many discrepancies in the vocabulary levels of your students and the effects these have on them. We share your concerns. All students deserve to be involved in a vocabulary program that not only helps them learn words of value to them, but provides them with direction in how to learn those words in the most efficient and meaningful manner.

The purpose of this book is to help you reflect on the effectiveness of your own vocabulary program while examining new information and processes that might help you become more effective. Our hope is that as you consider new ways to teach vocabulary, you will gain greater insight into how the vocabulary size of students can be increased and how to increase the number of strategies your students use to determine or refine the meaning of new words. This book should also help you understand the differences between how younger and older students learn new words and how to use research-based strategies effectively in your classroom.

Our belief is that if you strengthen your vocabulary program, you will not only be able to reduce the gap between learners with poor word knowledge versus those with robust word knowledge, but you will also create an environment where all students value the power of words. In both ways, you will improve everyone's chances of success in school and in life.

Before turning to the next chapter, reflect on your current vocabulary program. Think about how you help students expand their vocabularies, and then score yourself on each of the self-reflection questions in Figure 1.4. As you continue to read this book, you will find information that relates to each of these questions. Our hope is that this book will help you consider changes you might like to make in the ways you treat and teach vocabulary in your classroom.

Figure 1.4.
Self-Reflection Questionnaire: Vocabulary Learning in My Classroom

How would you rate your current classroom practices for vocabulary instruction?

Indicate to what extent you do the following:

Do I focus on vocabulary learning in my classroom?

Small extent				Great extent
1	2	3	4	5

Do my students understand the value of vocabulary and how it affects their ability to read, write, and speak?

Small extent				Great extent
1	2	3	4	5

Do I use a robust vocabulary in the classroom?

Small extent				Great extent
1	2	3	4	5

Do I create a classroom setting that is vocabulary rich?

Small extent				Great extent
1	2	3	4	5

Do I engage students in wide reading experiences (sustained silent reading) as a means to build their vocabulary and background knowledge?

Small extent				Great extent
1	2	3	4	5

Do I have an established set of criteria based on current research that I use to make decisions about what words students will be learning?

Small extent				Great extent
1	2	3	4	5

Do I provide direct instruction on complex, abstract words?

Small extent				Great extent
1	2	3	4	5

Figure 1.4.
Self-Reflection Questionnaire: Vocabulary Learning in My Classroom *(continued)*

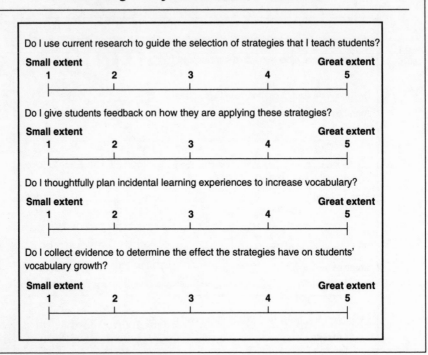

Do I use current research to guide the selection of strategies that I teach students?

Small extent   **Great extent**

1   2   3   4   5

Do I give students feedback on how they are applying these strategies?

Small extent   **Great extent**

1   2   3   4   5

Do I thoughtfully plan incidental learning experiences to increase vocabulary?

Small extent   **Great extent**

1   2   3   4   5

Do I collect evidence to determine the effect the strategies have on students' vocabulary growth?

Small extent   **Great extent**

1   2   3   4   5

The Developmental Aspects of Vocabulary Learning

In *The Phantom Tollbooth* (1971) by Norton Juster, a young boy named Milo wanders through Dictionopolis, a kingdom ruled by King Azar. As he enters the Word Market, he is amazed at the assortment of words for sale:

"Step right up, step right up—fancy, best-quality words right here," announced one man in a booming voice. "Step right up—ah, what can I do for you, little boy? How about a nice bagful of pronouns—or maybe you'd like our special assortment of names?"

Milo had never thought much about words before, but these looked so good that he longed to have some. . . .

"Maybe if I buy some I can learn how to use them," said Milo eagerly as he began to pick through the words in the stall. Finally he chose three which looked particularly good to him—"quagmire," "flabbergast," and "upholstery." He had no idea what they meant, but they looked very grand and elegant [p. 47].

Milo is lucky that he has a place to acquire new words. But most children just can't go to a market and buy words. So where do they go to learn new words? Does the source of these new words vary from one grade level to another? Do students acquire and require different types of words in different grade levels? Are there developmental differences in how children use strategies to learn new words?

This chapter answers these questions by providing an overview of the differences in how children acquire and use vocabulary from kindergarten until the end of sixth grade. To do this, we consider three aspects of vocabulary learning for the K–1, 2–3, and 4–6 grade spans and present the implications for setting up a vocabulary program in the elementary school: typical word knowledge, developing expanded vocabularies, and acquiring vocabulary strategies. Keep in mind that *these grade spans are artificial structures that we impose on children and that not all children fall neatly into them.*

KINDERGARTEN THROUGH FIRST GRADE
Typical Word Knowledge

The primary source of learning new words for young children during the first five years of their life is oral language experience: they learn new words because they hear them. As they begin to try out new words, they receive feedback on how to say and use the words correctly. Over time they come to understand what the words mean and how to use them appropriately. If children are consistently involved in rich and repeated give-and-take oral language experiences, they learn a great number of words.

In their early years, the words children are learning are those common to their own environment. For example, a child who is raised on a farm may be very well acquainted with the words *hayfield, sugar beet,* and *fertilizer.* A child from the city may not know the meaning of these words, but his vocabulary might include words like *theater, suburb,* and *light rail*—vocabulary that the child who lives on the farm may not yet have encountered.

As children enter kindergarten, the way they learn new words is not significantly different from how they learned new words before they entered school: they still learn most of their new words by ear rather than by sight. The context of learning and the very nature of the new words they are hearing start to change as children gradually move from everyday language to the "book" or "academic" language of school—a language that often uses different words and sentence structures than children are familiar with through their everyday conversations and experiences.

This oral approach typically continues into first grade. Children continue to learn words related to their experiences in and out of school, although they are increasingly adding content words that are important to the world of their class-room. For example, a teacher may plan a unit of instruction for a first-grade classroom about the planets and space where students would learn new words like *constellation, Milky Way,* and *orbit.* These may not be high-frequency words or words that students have been encountering at home, but they are important if students are going to be proficient in the curriculum of planets and space that has been designated as essential content in that school for the first grade.

Developing Expanded Vocabularies

It is well documented in the research literature that children as young as two and three years of age often make up new words by adding suffixes and prefixes by anal-ogy. If one can *un-plug* the TV, then it is possible to *un-color* a messed-up color-ing book. However, it is not until children acquire a certain level of understanding of how language operates (called meta-linguistic awareness) that they are able to understand the structure of a word and the function of the different parts of the word. For example, it is improbable that a kindergartner or first grader would un-derstand the following poem from *The Biology of Algae and Diverse Other Verses* by Ralph Lewin (1997) even though they think it sounds funny. An older child would be able to discern how certain words were derived from the previous word and why some made sense and others did not:

> *Though sinners sin*
> *And thinners thin*
> *And paper blotters blot;*
> *I've never yet*
> *Had letters let*
> *Or seen an otter ot* [p. 88].

Starting in first grade, children begin to be aware of commonly used prefixes and suffixes such as *pre-, re-,* and *–less.* It is easier for children to recognize a suffix when it is simply added to a root word without changing the way this root word is spelled or pronounced. For example, the relationships between the words *teach* and *teacher* or *hope* and *hopeful* are more transparent than the relationship within such pairs as *product* and *production* or *personal* and *personality.* It is also at this age that children become familiar with some commonly used inflections and know what they mean. For example, they can understand that adding *–ed* to a verb means that something was done in the past, and adding *–s* to a noun means dealing with several things instead of just one.

Most kindergartners and first-grade students are able to predict the meaning of compound words based on the known meaning of the words that make up this compound word. For example, knowing the words *rain* and *drop,* the child can correctly guess the meaning of the word *raindrop.*

Primary-grade students' ability to understand multiple meanings of a word is limited to the case when all of these meanings are the literal ones. In order to learn the multiple meanings of a word such as *fair,* students need direct instruction. Young children tend to interpret literally most idioms, metaphors, and proverbs they encounter. Nevertheless, they are able to understand figurative language and multiple meanings as long as the new meaning of the word is connected with the known meaning in a concrete fashion. For example, children learn words that describe various colors by using the name of an object exemplifying this color such as *lime, violet,* or *lavender.*

Acquiring Vocabulary Strategies

It is important to remember that young learners have not yet fully developed the awareness of what they know and what they do not know. As a result, they are not likely to interrupt a reader or a narrator with a question about a word they hear for the first time. If they do, it is typically not because they recognize that they are confused but rather because they are curious about something they are hearing about for the first time and want to know more about it. You cannot assume that at this age children will learn new words because they are confused and therefore ask about the meaning of the unknown word.

Because young children have low levels of language awareness, they are not used to defining words in the same formal way older children and adults do. Instead of defining a word taxonomically, that is, in terms of a larger class to which it belongs (such as defining *knife* as a *utensil* or *couch* as *furniture*), younger children tend to define a word using synonyms (an *ape* is a *monkey*), describing its functions (a *car* is something you ride in), or listing its attributes (a *bicycle* has two wheels that go around, metal bars, and a seat). This is a significant distinction to keep in mind when choosing dictionaries for young students. Look for dictionaries that contain concrete language and lots of pictures.

SECOND AND THIRD GRADES

Typical Word Knowledge

As students move into the end of first grade and on to second grade, the vocabulary they are learning becomes more directly related to the content they are learning in the classroom. They become much more aware that there are words they do not know and are more capable of asking questions about specific words. The read-aloud experiences they are having include many more words and concepts that extend beyond their typical everyday experiences outside school and continue to help them make the transition from learning words orally to learning words from the written texts. As they master the beginnings of reading, they start to use print as a source of learning new words; nevertheless, until they reach a high level of reading fluency, oral language remains their primary source of new words. This dependence on oral language probably explains why it is important for teachers and parents to continue reading aloud to second- and third-grade students. The vocabulary in the books adults read aloud to children at this age is more advanced than the vocabulary in the books children can read on their own. Therefore, read-aloud experiences offer more opportunities for important oral language experiences and vocabulary development.

At this time we see a huge discrepancy between students' reading vocabulary and their listening vocabulary. Books that students read at this stage are usually assigned to them based on their reading levels, which means that they are expected to know at least 85 percent of the words in a book. Consequently, the reading vocabulary of second and third graders typically is much more limited than their listening vocabulary.

Developing Expanded Vocabularies

In second and third grades, children continue to increase their vocabularies by adding new words derived from existing ones. By now, they can understand the meaning of words that have prefixes such as *un-, re-,* and *pre-* or suffixes such as *-er, -est, -ful,* and *-less* and can also explain what these prefixes and suffixes mean. They can determine the meaning of common compound words, such as *lunchroom* and *baseball,* by explaining the relationship between the words contained in the compound. Repeatedly encountering frequently used prefixes and suffixes in printed texts and in their own writing helps children solidify understanding of their functions in words.

As print gradually gains importance as a source of new words, children add new words to their vocabulary that exist in written form only: contractions and abbreviations. They are already familiar with the meaning of words such as *February* and *Wednesday,* so they can understand what *Feb.* and *Wed.* mean in context.

Second and third graders expand their knowledge of multiple meanings of words by learning new literal meanings and new figurative meanings. Their understanding of idiomatic language is still limited by the concreteness of the image evoked by the idiom or metaphor. A sign of children's ability to understand multiple meanings of a word is their growing interest in word play, puns, and jokes based on this semantic ambivalence.

Acquiring Vocabulary Strategies

By the time they are in first or second grade, children start asking questions about specific words. With their meta-linguistic awareness growing, they start asking questions not only about the meaning of new words (What is a *woodchuck?*) but also about the relationships between different words (Is a *woodchuck* an *animal?*). Children thus develop the ability to define new words in a more structured way that approximates the formal definitions used in dictionaries. In their definitions, children often go beyond describing the function of an object and begin to define it as a member of a larger category, for example, "A *diamond* is a *gem* that you put in a ring."

Being able to use taxonomic definitions makes it possible for second and third graders to understand how conventional dictionaries work. By now, children usually are fluent in using alphabetical order in searching for words, so using a dictionary becomes more practical.

By second grade, schooling begins to have a much stronger effect on vocabulary than in the earlier grades. It can be attributed not only to the new words being taught but also to learning new strategies about the use of context cues. Children are taught to use synonyms and other alternative words and phrases that express the same or similar meanings to extract meaning from a printed text and also to extend and enhance their own writing. As children use words such as *asked, whispered,* and *mumbled* as alternatives to *said,* they begin to understand that words may have similar denotations (literal meanings) and different connotations (nuances).

Children are also taught how to look for a familiar word inside an unfamiliar one as a part of a set of word attack skills they learn during their beginning stages of reading and writing instruction. While not a part of vocabulary instruction, word attack skills become a useful strategy to deal with derived words, setting the stage for morphological analysis, a more sophisticated strategy children will learn in the upper elementary grades.

FOURTH THROUGH SIXTH GRADES

Typical Word Knowledge

Toward the end of their elementary years, students typically have developed reading skills to the point that they can use print as a major source for learning new words. This is not to say that they do not learn new words orally, but the books they are reading often contain a higher density of new words than their conversations do. By this age, "conversation is not a substitute for reading" when it comes to vocabulary growth (Cunningham and Stanovich, 1998, p. 3).

The major vocabulary development in these upper grades focuses on challenging content-area vocabulary and more abstract words such as *assume, conclude,* and *hypothesize* that can apply to more than one content area. Students are most likely to learn and use these words if their teachers repeatedly use them across different subjects. In order to make print a valuable source for learning new words, the vocabulary of the assigned reading books needs to be ahead of children's everyday speaking and listening vocabulary. Much of the literature students choose to read at this age may contain some new words, but typically their independent reading is not the primary source of vocabulary learning. For example, it is estimated that a vocabulary size of only five thousand words is sufficient to read novels written for teenagers or younger readers (Hirsch and Nation, 1992).

Developing Expanded Vocabularies

By grade 4, students are developing increasing meta-linguistic awareness. They have also had some experience in studying word parts, usually in their spelling program. This understanding helps them prepare for the more formal analysis required for understanding words that have Greek or Latin roots, prefixes, or suffixes such as *tele-vision, tele-phone,* and *photo-graph.* To understand the meaning of these words and their structure, children need to have had some experience with using formal definitions in which words are defined through other words and out of context. With sufficient exposure to words of foreign origin in print, children learn to recognize these words using some of the frequent spelling patterns, such as the use of *ph* and not *f,* which in turn are used as a cue to apply knowledge of Greek or Latin roots.

Upper elementary students can use both the literal and figurative meanings of many words. However, it is still easier for them to use idioms and metaphors that are based on visual imagery and common knowledge than ones that have a more obscure base and are foreign to their own experiences. For example, *walking on thin ice* is an easier expression for children to understand than *spill the beans.* By the end of the upper elementary grades, many children understand commonly used idioms and metaphors. However, as is the case with vocabulary learning in general, they will always understand more words than they use (Levorato and Cacciari, 1995), and the gap is even wider for idioms and metaphors. It helps to know how children come to understand and use figurative language as you create opportunities for them to show off their knowledge of vocabulary, especially idioms and metaphors. Think carefully about the words and expressions you use in class; you might want to check to make sure your students, especially English Language Learners (ELL), understand what you're saying when you introduce an idiomatic expression such as "Hold your horses" or "It's a piece of cake."

Acquiring Vocabulary Strategies

In upper elementary grades, children are gradually gaining more independence in using strategies to determine word meaning, but they can struggle with knowing which strategy to use when. This often leads students to overrely on a single strategy (usually guessing the meaning of a word from the context), which becomes ineffective for texts with a high density of new words. Relying on context tends to backfire when it is applied to the abstract, technical, and academic words that start appearing in reading materials in grade 4 and beyond (Chall, Jacobs, and Baldwin, 1990).

By fifth and sixth grades, children have typically mastered the skill of formal definition and can use multiple sources to determine the meaning of a new word: dictionaries, glossaries, sidebars, footnotes, and others. However, their ability to use formal definitions may not reach the adult levels without explicit modeling and coaching by teachers, followed by practice in defining the words (Kurland and Snow, 1997).

SECOND LANGUAGE LEARNERS

The developmental patterns in learning vocabulary generally apply to students whose native language is not English. Nevertheless, within these patterns, there may be variations from those we have already described in this chapter.

Typical Word Knowledge

Unless your school has a special bilingual program, ELL students are likely to have to learn how to read English at the same time they are mastering the oral language. In this, they are different from English-speaking students who build on their listening and speaking vocabulary before making the transition to print as the major source of new words. In addition, ELL students are not likely to have some of the opportunities English-speaking students have to expand their oral vocabulary because many of them do not speak English at home. Therefore, at least in the beginning, ELL students might have difficulties understanding books that you read aloud in class.

The major cause for potential academic difficulties ELL students face is their slow acquisition of academic vocabulary even when these students seem to make good progress in learning everyday vocabulary. Systematic vocabulary instruction can significantly minimize the gap between English-speaking and ELL students if this instruction starts early and is delivered over several years (Lesaux and Siegel, 2003).

Developing Expanded Vocabularies

For the reasons described, ELL students may have a particularly hard time when encountering idiomatic expressions and words with multiple meanings. Therefore, they benefit from more explicit explanations and more examples than you would use with English-speaking students.

ELL students whose native language is similar in structure to English may expand their vocabularies by inferring the meaning of unfamiliar English words based on their knowledge of cognates—words that sound similar to English in their native language and have similar meaning. For example, whether a student knows the meaning of the Spanish word *identidad,* the French word *identité,* the Italian word *identitá,* or the Portuguese word *identidade,* this student is likely to guess the meaning of the English word *identity* correctly. Words like these are more often helpful in content areas than in everyday conversations.

Acquiring Vocabulary Strategies

ELL students who come to the classroom with large vocabularies (or even the beginnings of literacy) in their native language may soon develop higher levels of meta-linguistic awareness than their English-speaking classmates. Having to constantly switch between languages makes ELL students more aware of the structure of words and their meanings. This awareness may assist them in learning specific vocabulary strategies. Students with limited vocabularies in their native language will need more explicit and more extensive instruction in vocabulary strategies.

IMPLICATIONS FOR AN EFFECTIVE VOCABULARY PROGRAM

Certainly, there are differences in how students learn vocabulary from kindergarten through sixth grade. In order to ensure that your vocabulary program addresses the developmental needs of all of your students, we make the following recommendations:

• *An effective vocabulary program should create a seamless transition from learning words orally to learning words from the written text.* Initially, in kindergarten and first grade, oral vocabulary is the leading source for learning new words. A heavy emphasis should be placed on using oral language to promote vocabulary learning in these grades. Increased and more thoughtful emphasis should be placed on how students encounter unknown words through their reading experiences as they move from second through sixth grades.

• *An effective vocabulary program should help students make the transition from the vocabulary they are learning at home to content-area vocabulary that supports increasingly sophisticated curriculum.* There is a rather predictable order in which students learn new words, whether they are learning them orally or from the written text. This order depends on several factors such as word size, word frequency, the degree to which the word denotes a progressively more abstract or complex concept, and the degree to which the word relates to content within various curriculum subjects (such as science, social studies, or math).

Before children begin school, they have a strong need for vocabulary that is basic to their everyday lives. As they progress through elementary school, this need is overshadowed by the need for a more school-oriented vocabulary—one that is more content based, increasingly more complex and abstract, and applies to more than one content area. A strong vocabulary program should reflect the transition between these two sources, moving in the very early grades from the home-oriented vocabulary to one that has a strong emphasis on increasingly complex content-area vocabulary.

• *An effective vocabulary program should allow students to learn new words based on words they are already familiar with.* Children expand their vocabulary by adding various forms to words they already know. It is hypothesized that it is the ability to learn how new words are derived from known words that accounts for the fact that between grades 1 and 5, children increase their vocabulary size from approximately ten thousand words to approximately forty thousand (Anglin, 1993). For example, children can fairly accurately guess the meaning of the word *unstoppable* if they know the word *stop* and the meaning of other words that have *un-* or *–able* in them. They also expand their vocabularies by learning new meanings of known words. You can think of these as words that have separate entries in the dictionary such as the word *fair,* which has one meaning as a noun and several as an adjective.

Understanding multiple meanings of words is not only important for children's successful academic performance in school, it is also critical for their social functioning. It was estimated that 36 percent of all utterances produced by teachers from kindergarten through grade 8 contained at least one multimeaning statement (Lazar, Warr-Leeper, Nicholson, and Johnson, 1989). That is why it is important to reflect on your own use of language, especially with children who have limited vocabularies and with the ELL students. Suppose you are trying to let a group of children know that they are close to understanding some new piece of content and you use the expression, "You're in the ballpark." If the children know only that a ballpark is where a sports game is played, they will not understand what you mean.

• *An effective vocabulary program should enable students to learn and use vocabulary strategies.* Depending on the source and type of new words being learned, children use different strategies to determine, refine, and remember the meaning of new words. The strategies children employ to derive meaning from oral sources are different from the ones needed to understand words encountered in the written texts.

As children develop more advanced cognitive and language competencies, they tend to develop more sophisticated strategies for learning unknown words. Some children develop useful strategies on their own, while others remain somewhat deficient in this area. A lack of the use of effective strategies impairs their understanding of the meaning of the unknown word. In addition to strategies for comprehending, students need strategies to help them remember the new word so they will be able to use it in speaking and writing. A typical strategy students use for this is to write the word down multiple times. This is not the most effective strategy. A meta-analysis of current research states that one of the most effective ways to learn a new word is to associate an image with it (Marzano, Pickering, and Pollock, 2001).

The degree to which children use strategies independently to tease out the meaning of a word, build on their knowledge of known words, and identify subtle differences among similar words increases as they develop rich, robust vocabularies. Teachers should model the use of strategies identified by research that have the greatest effect on student learning, provide students time to apply these strategies, and give students feedback on their progress. As students move from primary to upper elementary grade levels, instruction in how to use these strategies should move from a very teacher-directed approach to a more independent or student-directed approach.

• *An effective vocabulary program should provide additional support for ELL students in mastering oral and written English.* The specific kind of support ELL students need will depend on many factors, including their age, their proficiency in English, the language they speak at home, and whether they have developed a large vocabulary in their native language that includes academic concepts. An effective vocabulary program is flexible enough to accommodate the diverse needs of ELL students by providing them with additional support.

Most of the strategies discussed in this book work equally well for students who speak English and for ELL students; however, ELL students may require more practice in using these strategies and may also require more explicit explanations than their English-speaking peers.

SUMMARY

As a classroom teacher, it is important for you to have an understanding of the impact of age differences on vocabulary development because these differences have clear implications for establishing an effective vocabulary program. In Chapters Three, Four, and Five, we help you apply this developmental understanding to the variety of approaches you can use to teach vocabulary.

Understanding Approaches to Teaching Vocabulary

A group of sixth-grade teachers in Louisiana has spent three years pursuing a wide reading program (sometimes called sustained silent reading) in which students are encouraged to read books of their own choice for a period of time each day. The teachers initially thought this could serve as a major vehicle for enhancing students' vocabulary, but they have not seen the growth they hoped for and are not quite sure why. They don't want to abandon the program because students are involved in and enjoying reading more than ever before. Yet they feel that they need to be doing more with vocabulary.

One afternoon, as they discussed this challenge in their team meeting, they realized that vocabulary instruction across their various classrooms was somewhat disjointed. Typically, they independently decided which words were important for students to learn, yet there were several commonalities in how they selected the words. For example, they all selected words from the literature students were reading and from the content students were learning in the various subject areas. But major differences existed among the criteria they applied to select words and the amount of time each teacher spent on vocabulary instruction. One teacher selected high-frequency words, while another picked words she thought would be interesting to students. A third teacher focused on vocabulary instruction at least two or three times a day, while another gave his students ten new words each week, provided no instruction, and gave a test on the definitions every Friday. After some discussion, the teachers

23

decided that they would like to work together to create a more cohesive and focused program across their grade level.

Their team leader, Mr. King, suggested that they collectively create a sixth-grade vocabulary list that was in line with the content their students would be learning and contained words students needed for general reading proficiency. The team liked Mr. King's idea, so they set about gathering their resources and soon created a customized list. But now that they had it, they weren't sure what to do with it. They wondered how they could possibly find enough time in their full schedules to teach all of these words.

As they discussed what they might do, one teacher said that he had heard that one of the primary ways that students learn new words is through incidental learning experiences, but he wasn't quite sure what that meant. He did feel, however, that a major reason there were so many differences in the vocabulary levels of his students was that some students had many and varied experiences outside school where they were exposed to new words and concepts while others did not.

Another teacher suggested there was some controversy surrounding direct instruction—that there is not enough time in the school day to directly teach all of the words that students need to learn, so there was little value in direct instruction. Still another pointed out that different words require different levels of understanding; they shouldn't treat all words the same. Given all these conflicting viewpoints, the teachers were not clear about what their next steps should be.

At this point, you too may be wondering how to implement the most effective vocabulary program. If you have to provide students with appropriate learning experiences for all of the words on your list, how can you possibly carve out enough time? How can you integrate wide reading, incidental learning experiences, and direct instruction to build an effective vocabulary program in your classroom? That is what we address in this chapter. We begin with the various approaches to teaching vocabulary, which include the following student needs:

- Engage in multiple learning experiences
- Understand how vocabulary learning relates to their success in reading and writing

- Engage in direct instruction
- Engage in well-planned incidental learning experiences

OFFERING MULTIPLE LEARNING EXPERIENCES

Just seeing or hearing a word once will probably not be enough to help you understand and use that word (unless it has quite a critical impact on you). The same is true for children. They need multiple exposures to words to be able to use them. In fact, some researchers have found that students need to be exposed to a new word at least six times in a meaningful context in order to learn it (Jenkins, Stein, and Wysocki, 1984).

Sometimes these multiple encounters occur within the same context, and that is sufficient. For example, if a child was given a vitamin each morning before breakfast and was told, "Take your vitamin," the child would remember the word *vitamin* over a period of time and probably be able to respond, "Yes, I took my vitamin." Although the child might know the word *vitamin* and even be able to use the word, she may not know anything more than that it is a pill that is good for her and she should take it every day. In this case, the word was used multiple times but always in the same context, so she did not increase or extend her understanding of what the word meant, only her capacity to remember the word. Her conversations and experiences never progressed beyond just *"taking the vitamin,"* so her ability to use the word in other contexts is limited by her narrow understanding of what the word means.

For some words, this surface level of understanding is sufficient. Other words demand more understanding and thus require not only multiple encounters but a variety of contexts so that children come to understand the nuances of the word and build strong networks of related vocabulary. Ben learned about dinosaurs through multiple contexts—his toy, books, his grandmother, and television. He learned that dinosaurs are animals, but they are different from lions and dogs and pigs because they are extinct. This distinction makes dinosaurs different from all of the other animals Ben knows about. Ben's understanding of this distinction deepens his knowledge of his new word *extinct*. All of these oral experiences worked together to deepen his understanding of how a dinosaur is like and different from other animals. It also gave him additional vocabulary that he could use not only when he spoke about dinosaurs but also in other arenas where the words applied.

Each encounter that a kindergarten or first-grade student has with a new word is typically surrounded by a context. For example, young students are often treated to repeated readings of the same books or singing of the same familiar songs. Through this repetition, they come to know and remember new words. In the reading of these stories or the singing of the songs, the teacher or parent often provides facial expressions, comments, emotions, and even pictures that help students understand the new word.

As students progress through the grades, they no longer can rely on the context clues embodied in an oral language experience since they are moving toward a reading-based approach to vocabulary learning. They increasingly encounter complex content-area words through the assigned readings selected for their grade level. Students' ability to accurately understand these content words and use them depends on their understanding of the underlying concepts related to the new vocabulary.

Because students in the upper grades are reading more difficult books with more new content, the assumption is that they will be learning more new words because they are encountering more unknown words. There has been much discussion of how wide reading or sustained silent reading will help develop a child's vocabulary. However, unless students encounter the unknown word multiple times while reading, they may not have significant increases in their vocabulary levels. As you think about how students will learn new words in your classroom, you need to consider the number of encounters, the contexts surrounding these encounters, and the effects these encounters will have on the level of understanding and extended network of words that students have already developed or need to develop.

RELATING VOCABULARY TO SUCCESS IN READING AND WRITING

Students may not understand that having a strong vocabulary helps them be better readers and writers. But the more words and concepts they know, the greater the chance is that they will be successful at learning new information (Marzano, 2004). Their background knowledge helps them interpret and make sense of new information, so if they have limited or no background knowledge, it is difficult for them to construct meaning around the new information they are receiving. Having a strong vocabulary increases students' background knowledge, which not only helps them learn new information but helps them be better readers and writers. Students need to understand the link between vocabulary, reading, and writing.

Students also need to understand that writers use words to convey what they want to say accurately and vividly. It is important for you to help students understand the meaningful relationship between the reader and the writer. The following are some examples of experiences teachers provided their students to help them gain this understanding.

One Little Word

Ms. Ohashi wants her class to see the difference that a single word can make to the meaning of a sentence, so she writes the following sentence stem on the chalkboard and asks the children to fill in the blank: *Bubbles are* _____.

As each child responds, she writes the word in the blank, placing additional responses underneath the previous response. Katrina suggests the word *awesome,* while Emmanuelle describes her bubble as *drippy.* The class discusses whether a bubble can be *awesome* and *drippy* at the same time. Ms. Ohashi asks the children to consider a bubble that is *drippy* and *slippery.* With each new sentence, Ms. Ohashi has the children close their eyes and create a mental picture of each sentence. Then she gives each child a sheet of paper on which to write his or her own words describing bubbles. She tries to impress on students the importance of choosing words that convey what they want to say accurately and vividly.

Liven It Up!

Mr. Slaughter gives students a deliberately dull passage with certain words underlined (Exhibit 3.1). He challenges the students to change just the underlined words to make the story more interesting and exciting. Students work in small groups to complete the assignment. Their rewritten paragraphs are always lively and as different from each other as they are from the original dull paragraph. Mr. Slaughter talks to students about the differences the choice of words makes and the effect on readers. He helps students understand that words really do make a difference.

Let's Revise

The stories Mr. Hoogerdijk's students write are filled with ordinary and overused words. To help them understand the effect these words have on readers, he pairs students together and has them read their stories to each other. After reading the story, the reader is asked to describe how the words helped create a mental picture of what was going on in the story. As students begin to share their experience as a

---

Exhibit 3.1.
Example of a Dull Paragraph and Revisions

_We_ _went_ to the _store_ in our car to _buy_ _things_. Along the way, we saw _an_ _animal_ _running_ _fast_ after another _animal_. When we _got_ _to_ _the_ _store_, we saw _someone_ _walking_ in the door. We _walked_ around the _store_ together and _bought_ _nice_ _things_.

We _motored_ to the _grocery_ _store_ in our _Porsche_ to _purchase_ _household_ _items_. Along the way, we saw _a_ _dingo_ _charging_ _after_ _a_ _wild_ _cat_. When we finally arrived, we saw _a store_ _detective_ _pacing_ in front of the _revolving_ _door_. We _scurried_ _around_ the _aisles_ together and purchased _exquisite_ _items_.

_My_ _brother_ _and_ _I_ _rushed_ to the _sports_ _mall_ in our _Jeep_ to _lease_ _some_ _climbing_ _gear_. Along the way, we saw a _Doberman_ _cavorting_ _with_ _a_ porcupine. When we _appeared_ _at_ _the_ _sports_ _mall_, we saw _John_ _Elway_ _sauntering_ through the _automatic_ door. We _scurried_ _through_ _the_ _maze_ _of_ _sports_ _equipment_ together and _gathered_ _the_ _items_ _we_ _needed_.

---

class, they see that their use of ordinary and overused words makes it difficult for the reader to create the same vivid mental picture that the writer had wanted to portray. Mr. Hoogerdijk then has students make a list of these ordinary and overused words and places them for all students to see. Students are then asked to go back to their writing and change these words. Students share their revisions with their partners. The partners are asked to listen specifically for new words and create mental pictures as they listen. Then they are asked to share any new images or understandings and discuss how the new vocabulary makes the story more inviting.

Newsworthy Words

At the beginning of the school year, Mrs. Decker has her students bring in newspaper articles of interest to them. She explains that when you don't know the meaning of the words, it is difficult to understand what you read. She asks students to list the words in their article that they do not know. Mrs. Decker writes the words on the chalkboard and then gives a brief explanation of what the unknown words mean and has the students read the article again. After they are finished, she asks them how knowing the meaning of the words affected their ability to understand the article. She explains that knowing the meaning of an unknown word may be critical to comprehension and that throughout the rest of the year, they will be learning strategies to increase their capacity to figure out the meaning of unknown words.

Vocabulary Predictions

Ms. Pettit wants her students to understand that vocabulary can be used to help them set a purpose for reading. She uses *Just Grandpa and Me,* a fairly simple book, to demonstrate a strategy called "Probable Passages" (Wood, 1984). She selects some of the vocabulary in the book and, using the graphic organizer shown in Figure 3.1, asks students to make predictions as to what they think the book is about. Once students complete making their predictions, she asks them what they want to do next. The students overwhelmingly state that they want to read the book to find out if their predictions are true.

Figure 3.1.
The Probable Passages Strategy

Just Grandpa and Me

Vocabulary Terms and Phrases		
department store	chopsticks	scary
revolving	ticket agent	soy sauce
escalator	wok	rail

Setting	
Characters	
Problem	
Events	
Ending	

After Ms. Pettit reads the book to students, they discuss their predictions and the degree to which they are accurate. She encourages students to discuss how using the vocabulary helped them want to read the book and also helped them access their prior knowledge. She helps students understand that they can use this strategy independently as they prepare to read a new book.

PLANNING FOR DIRECT INSTRUCTION

A teacher who thoughtfully and systematically engages students in specific steps and strategies that help them learn new words well enough to use them independently is using *direct instruction*. Words that require more extensive and deep-rooted understanding, either because they have multiple meanings or are very content specific, require direct instruction.

As students encounter more abstract and complex vocabulary, their need for direct instruction increases, which requires the teacher to carve out time to do this. Since instructional time is very precious, the selection of the strategies and words that are taught is very important. It would make no sense to pick words that are not important words or words that students could learn very easily on their own. Nor would it make sense to leave students to their own devices to develop strategies when research provides such a rich resource to draw from. Direct instruction provides a structure for teachers to intentionally plan for students to be engaged in at least six encounters with that word so that the student will have sufficient understanding of the word to use it both orally and in writing.

Direct instruction has four goals:

1. Provide a specified period of time for students to learn words that would be difficult for them to learn on their own but that are important to their success in school.

2. Provide teachers a period of time to model the use of effective vocabulary learning strategies.

3. Provide students time to apply these strategies to the important words they are learning.

4. Create a setting where students receive feedback and evaluate how effective they are in using these strategies to learn new words.

Setting aside time for modeling strategies for vocabulary learning during direct instruction is a key element of a strong vocabulary program. If teachers do not model vocabulary learning strategies, some students will develop their own and become proficient in using them. These are typically students who already have a strong vocabulary and tend to be very successful in school. Students who have a limited vocabulary, however, may not move beyond using the strategy of guessing the meaning of a new word. This may be useful in some situations, but if students do not move beyond guessing to using strategies to verify their guess, their vocabulary will not increase at a rate necessary to assist these students in comprehending and mastering subject matters.

Perhaps one reason that Mr. King's team was not seeing the results they wanted in their wide reading program was that students were not developing their capacity to use strategies for learning unknown words because the teachers were not spending time teaching strategies. In addition, many of the students with small vocabularies were selecting books that contained mostly familiar words and therefore were not encountering many new words. Some educators argue that since a major goal of wide reading is that students read for enjoyment and are more motivated to read when they can select their own materials, this is just fine. But we think that you can set up wide reading experiences that motivate students to read and that support them in increasing their vocabulary. In any case, if there is no direct instruction of vocabulary in the classroom, low-performing students are less likely to become proficient in the use of vocabulary learning strategies. In Chapter Four, we present a process and strategies for direct instruction.

PLANNING FOR INCIDENTAL LEARNING EXPERIENCES

It is important to engage students in multiple experiences to help them discover the meaning of a new word and make it part of their vocabulary. Typically, there are two means by which this might happen: incidental learning experiences and direct instruction. In this section, we deal with the incidental learning experiences.

Many teachers think that they have little control over students' incidental learning experiences. But we believe that they can plan and capitalize on these experiences. Incidental learning experiences can be separated into two types. One we will refer to as *random incidental learning experiences:* incidental learning experiences that the teacher has no control over. For example, a child who goes to the hardware store with her parents may see different kinds of tools, such as a *buzz saw,* a *table saw,* and a *hacksaw.* As her mother searches for a particular type of blade, the child asks the mother the names of the different saws and their purposes. As the mother describes what a buzz saw is and how it works, the child laughs as she hears the name. It reminds her of the noise that a bee makes, and she finds that quite funny. Knowing what a buzz saw is can be useful, but it is probably not a word that the child will encounter in the elementary school classroom.

The second type we will refer to as *planned incidental learning experiences.* In most cases, teachers can exercise some control over the incidental learning experiences students encounter at school. That is, many of the activities and structures already available in the classroom can contribute to incidental learning if they are well planned. You can thoughtfully create and plan specific learning experiences in which students will encounter words multiple times throughout the school year. These planned learning experiences do not involve direct instruction, but rather are meaningfully set in the context of everyday life in the classroom.

As a teacher, you should thoughtfully consider how you create the conditions for planned incidental learning to happen in your classroom. For example, as Christie Hutchins looked around her classroom, she noticed that it was rather barren when it came to vocabulary. She had a lot of books in the reading corner, but beyond that, there was little evidence that she thought that vocabulary was important. She was now considering what she would need to do to create an environment that would support various incidental learning experiences. Her first idea was to place books and resources strategically around the room to help create an atmosphere conducive to vocabulary learning. Christie has the right idea: she knows that creating a plan will ensure that her students have ample opportunity to encounter these words multiple times even if she is not quite sure how to move forward. In Chapter Five, we present strategies for planning the incidental learning experiences in your classroom.

SUMMARY

In this chapter, our goal was to help you reflect on the approaches to teaching vocabulary that you might be using in your classroom. To do this, it is important to consider the following:

- Students need to be engaged in multiple opportunities to learn a new word. The degree to which the word is complex and essential to the classroom experience will determine how extensive these opportunities need to be.

- A student's ability to read and write is tremendously affected by her vocabulary knowledge. As a teacher, you need to spend time helping students understand this relationship. Then you must consider how to use vocabulary as a means to increase students' comprehension while reading and their capacity to deliver their message while writing.

- Direct instruction is a powerful vehicle for helping students learn more complex vocabulary.

- Well-planned incidental learning experiences can produce increased vocabulary learning.

In the next two chapters, we will examine direct instruction and planned incidental learning of new vocabulary words in depth.

A Framework and Strategies for Direct Instruction

Mr. Coronado, a fifth-grade teacher, was thinking about using direct instruction for teaching new vocabulary words. As he reflected on the effectiveness of his current vocabulary program, he realized that he taught only two strategies for learning new words: context clues and dictionary use. He knew that he had clear expectations about which words his students should be learning but didn't know many strategies. He wondered what other strategies he should be modeling. When he stopped to really think about it, he wasn't quite sure what the explicit goals of direct instruction should be.

Setting aside time for direct instruction is important because students need structure to help them learn more difficult words. Direct instruction provides an opportunity to model vocabulary learning strategies using a clear set of steps. You simply cannot assume that students know how to learn a new word, especially if the word is complex or abstract. Complex vocabulary requires that students have multiple (at least six) encounters to develop the breadth of understanding necessary to be able to use the new word. At least one of these encounters should require students to associate a mental image or symbolic representation with their new word in order to tie a nonlinguistic representation to the linguistic understanding that the student is developing. Learning is much more powerful when these two systems—the linguistic and the nonlinguistic—interact. Direct instruction can and should meet these demands.

We suggest using these six concrete steps for learning every new word:

Step 1: The teacher identifies the new word and elicits students' background knowledge.

Step 2: The teacher explains the meaning of the new word.

Step 3: Students generate their own explanations, and the teacher helps clear up confusion or misinformation.

Step 4: Students create a visual representation of the new word.

Step 5: Students engage in experiences that deepen their understanding of the new word.

Step 6: Students engage in vocabulary games and activities to help them remember the word and its meaning.

Note that this set of steps represents the combined efforts of both teacher and students. For example, the first two steps in this process are typically led by the teacher, but there is an expectation that students provide prior knowledge related to the word, ask clarifying questions, or add explanations. In steps 3 through 6, there is an expectation that the teacher will clear up confusion or misconceptions, model strategies students might use to complete these steps, and provide students with feedback on their use of the strategies. Students may be involved in cooperative groups for sharing their understandings, clarifying misconceptions, or explaining how effective they were at applying a new strategy. It is a good idea to provide students with a copy of the steps, and as you introduce them, point out that engaging in this process is a collaborative experience of interaction between teacher and students.

Initially as you present this process to students, explain to them that these are steps they will engage in during the time set aside for direct instruction. They should come to understand that as they become more familiar with and gain more experience with this process, they will develop a repertoire of strategies they can use to learn words more independently.

Just as a reminder, students should not have to spend a great deal of time on each word. You may need to remind them that this is not art class; when they create symbolic representations or pictorial representations of their new words, for example, they need not create a masterpiece.

In this chapter, we explain the six steps in the process and present specific strategies students might use to become more proficient in each step. Remember that it is important to present a variety of strategies rather than to overuse a few and risk students' losing interest in learning new words. As you select a strategy to introduce to students, determine the degree to which your students are capable of engaging in this strategy if you model it, give them sufficient time to practice it, and receive timely feedback on their progress. Younger children need more teacher guidance and are less able than older children to engage in the strategies independently, but they are capable of engaging in most of the strategies we have identified.

As you read the next section, you will notice that we identify strategies only for steps 3 through 6 since steps 1 and 2 are teacher led. Our assumption is that as you present steps 3 through 6, you will model strategies students might use while engaging in these steps. Initially, and especially with young children, the use of these strategies will be very teacher directed. Over time, students should be able to use the strategies independently.

STEP 1: TEACHER IDENTIFIES NEW WORD AND ELICITS BACKGROUND KNOWLEDGE

An important part of learning is to tap into students' prior knowledge and experiences. There may be students in your classroom who have some information about or understanding of a new word. By asking them before presenting the meaning of the word, you are able to acknowledge their experiences and reinforce the importance of learning new words. They may also be able to offer some interesting contexts for the word that would help other students. For example, suppose that you were introducing the math term *area model*. Students may not have heard this word before, but they may have some understanding of what a *model* is or what *area* means. These understandings will help them as they try to understand the term *area model*.

STEP 2: TEACHER EXPLAINS THE MEANING OF THE NEW WORD

Initially, it is important to help students understand what a new word means. This needs to be done in such a way that children make sense of the new word in the context of something they are already familiar with or that will make sense to them.

This can be accomplished by telling students a story, giving them an explanation, providing a description in written or verbal form, or providing examples or nonexamples. For instance, you might present the following explanation or description of the meaning of the word *area model:*

> *Area model:* A technique mathematicians use to represent the chances of something occurring.

The explanation by itself may be somewhat confusing to students, so to help them gain further understanding, you tell them that you will use *area* (a concept that most upper elementary students are familiar with) to *model* the chances of Hector and Lenny picking colored chips if they were picking red and blue chips individually or together. One model will be used to represent the chance that Hector would have of drawing a red chip from a bag that has five blue and five red chips. The second area model will be used to represent the chance that Lenny would have of drawing a red chip. The third area model shows both boys' chances of picking chips of the same or different colors when they draw simultaneously. Providing students with a graphic representation can further their understanding of the term or concept as in Figure 4.1.

Keep in mind that the goal of this step is to provide students with a clear understanding of the meaning of the new word quickly and efficiently. This is particularly important because most words tagged for direct instruction often represent concepts that students are unfamiliar with or confused about.

STEP 3: STUDENTS GENERATE THEIR OWN EXPLANATIONS

Once you have completed the first two steps of the process, ask students to elaborate on the information they have been given independently or in small groups, and create their own descriptions or explanations of the meaning of the new word. They should have lots of flexibility in how they go about this; however, you cannot assume that they will know how to do this on their own. They will need to be taught a variety of strategies to help them generate their explanation. It will be important for you as a teacher to model how to use these strategies and provide feedback on the students' efforts. Ask them to reflect on how the strategy is helping them learn the new word. If students are having difficulty with this step, it is usually because they have little understanding of the meaning of the word or have no strategies to help them describe what they do understand.

Figure 4.1.
Visual Representation of an Area Model

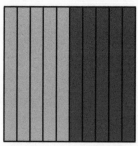

Hector's chances of drawing a red chip from a bag of 5 blue and 5 red chips are 5:10.

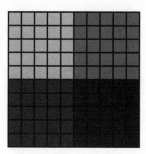

Lenny's chances of drawing a red chip from a bag of 5 blue and 5 red chips are 5:10.

Chances of both Hector and Lenny drawing a red chip from a bag of 5 blue and 5 red chips are 25:100.

Note: In the top diagram, the gray-stripped area represents the chances of Hector's drawing a red chip from a bag of five blue and five red chips. In the middle diagram, the gray-stripped area similarly represents Lenny's chances of drawing a red chip from a bag of five blue and five red chips. In the bottom diagram, the gray-stripped area represents the chances of both Hector and Lenny drawing a red chip from a bag of five blue and five red chips.

Here we look at two strategies that students can use:

- Using sentence stems or questions to describe the meaning of a word
- Using tools to learn more about a new word

Strategy: Using Sentence Stems or Questions to Describe the Meaning of a Word

Sentence stems may be the best strategy to help younger children think about the word they are trying to define. When young students define words, they do so by listing attributes, coming up with examples, or providing synonyms, so the stems will need to include these options—for example:

"I think this word means . . . that a thing is [does] . . . or . . . "

"We use this word to describe . . . , . . . , and . . . "

"We use this word when we want to say . . . "

Keep the questions for primary students relatively short and simple, so that children will be more likely to stay on topic—for example, ask:

"What does it mean that something *freezes?*"

"What do you know that *freezes?*"

Asking a question that allows many possible answers might lead classroom discussion in a direction that is off target. For example, asking, "Does this word remind you of something that happened to you?" might take the focus off the meaning of the target word. Young students are not used to providing verbal explanations of a target word. Therefore, as you ask questions about vocabulary, point to the objects on a picture or demonstrate an action that will go with a target word—for example:

"In this picture, are there any things that might *freeze?*"

"If it says that she *froze,* what would it look like? Can you *freeze* and run at the same time?"

For older students, the questions might be organized around memory cues and questions (Underwood, 1969). These sorts of questions will help students think about places, sounds, smells, emotions, events, or occasions that remind them of or are connected to the new word they are learning. Answering the questions helps to deepen their understanding of the new word and make it easier for them to create their own explanation of what the new word means. Figure 4.2 shows how a student learning the new term *dynasty* might answer the questions about the word.

Answering these questions will help students create nonlinguistic representations (such as sounds, smells, and emotions) to aid them in recalling the new word that they are learning. As a teacher reviews this student's chart, she should be able to help the student clear up his misunderstandings.

Exhibit 4.1 describes what the teacher is doing to support older students in learning the word *deforestation*. Notice how she combines the use of cues and questions to help students think about what they already know about the term being introduced and gives them an opportunity to think about the term at a deeper level.

Strategy: Using Tools to Learn More About a New Word

There are many resources, such as the thesaurus, the dictionary, and the Internet, that will provide students with additional information they can use to create their own definition of a word or clarify their understanding. Students need to be aware of these resources and how they might best use them to deepen their understanding of a new word.

Using a Dictionary.   The wonderful thing about dictionaries is that they can be used for different purposes and, when used correctly, can open up a whole new world for students. Students can use dictionaries to check the spelling of a word, learn new words, learn meanings of words, or find the right word to use in the right situation. They can also help students find how many syllables are in a word, figure out how to sound out a word, decide where the inflection goes on a word, what part of speech the word is, and how to use the word in a sentence. Since root words and word derivations can be very useful in helping students learn the meaning of a new word, older children should have access to dictionaries that contain Old English, Greek, and Latin derivations of words.

By the time most students have reached the fourth or fifth grade, they have had many experiences using a dictionary. They know the dictionary is an alphabetical listing of words that is divided into sections with guide words at the top. They understand alphabetical order to the second and third letter, necessary when using

Figure 4.2.
Student Responses to Teacher Questions About a New Word

Vocabulary Term: *dynasty*

Question	Response
Can you think of any places that you associate with this word?	Chinese palaces museums England — queen
Can you think of any sounds that you associate with this word?	trumpet — like king would hear when he entered room
Can you think of any smells that you associate with this word?	smell of money — rich people
Can you think of any emotions that you associate with this word?	excitement I would be scared to meet these people
Can you think of any events or occasions that you associate with this word?	Crowning of new king or leader

My explanation: *A powerful family that has ruled for many years. Power passes through family.*

Exhibit 4.1.
Teacher Questions About a New Word

Show students a visual of a rain forest that is tropical and protected.

Explain to students that they will be learning about deforestation with respect to rain forests and the negative effects this has on the world.

Questions

1. What do you think of when you think of rain forests?

2. What benefits do rain forests offer?

3. What are some ways deforestation occurs? (Slash and burn for agricultural purposes, commercial logging, etc.)

4. What are some causes? (Competitive global economy drives the need for money in economically challenged tropical countries, governments sell logging concessions to raise money for projects, to pay international debt, to develop industry, construct towns, etc.)

5. When do you consider deforestation to be a "good" idea?

6. When do you consider deforestation to be a "bad" idea?

7. Explain how the loss of rain forests will have a negative impact on the world.

8. If you were in charge of the world, what would you do to protect rain forests from commercial deforestation?

guide words to help locate key words. They also know the sections of a dictionary and how to read and use the guides provided in the dictionary.

Dictionaries work best when students already have some understanding of the word they are learning. There is, after all, no guarantee that when students look up a word in a dictionary, they will select the correct definition, pronounce that word correctly, and use it correctly in a sentence. However, with careful, explicit modeling and practice, students can learn how to use a dictionary to open the world of vocabulary.

As we pointed out in Chapter Two, younger children do not define words in the same formal ways adults do, that is, by using taxonomy and defining features. Instead, they define words by examples, by function, and by using words that are close in their meaning to the target one. However, even if primary students do not find traditional dictionaries very helpful, they can use special children's dictionaries that have concrete language and often contain pictures. A useful skill primary students need to acquire is how to use alphabetical order to make word search most efficient.

Using a Thesaurus.   There are two ways a thesaurus can be organized: by category and by alphabetical order. Students should know how to use both types and to decide when to use which thesaurus based on the work they are doing and their preference as a learner.

When students use a thesaurus in writing, they look at synonyms for the word they are trying to replace. Therefore, it is important that they have a good understanding of that word and how it fits in the sentence they are composing. This knowledge will help them avoid selecting a word that just does not make sense in that sentence.

When students use a thesaurus to look up synonyms for words, they should know the correct definition of the word. Steps 1 and 2 of the process set out in this chapter help them establish some understanding of what the new word means. They can then use the thesaurus to help them make distinctions between their word and the accompanying synonyms.

A thesaurus is good for helping students find new words to replace words they use too often. The exercise of using a thesaurus will reinforce the message that vocabulary is important to writers because it helps them communicate the exact message or information they wish to relate.

Using the Internet and Other Electronic Sources.   The same rules apply to using online dictionaries and thesauruses as apply to using the printed ones, but electronic tools call for even more caution since the ease of searching for and replacing words on the computer often leads students to use these tools mindlessly. Teach students not to use electronic tools in the Replace All mode (when all misspelled or selected words are automatically replaced). They would not want to find themselves in the position of one fifth grader who, when writing a report about Elizabeth I, replaced a misspelled word *virgin* (which he was not familiar with) with a similar-looking word from a spellchecker, which led to Queen Elizabeth's being named a "Vegan Queen"!

STEP 4: STUDENTS CREATE VISUAL REPRESENTATIONS

This step encourages students to translate what they have been learning about the new word into an image: a mental picture, symbol, graphic organizer, physical representation, or kinesthetic representation. In order to do this, students must think about their current understanding of the meaning of the word and then depict that meaning in a certain way. Creating a visual representation forces students to process their linguistic understanding into a nonlinguistic representation. If they have limited understanding of the meaning of the word, they will find it very difficult to create a visual representation, and this is a clue to students that they need to gain more understanding about the meaning of the word. Visual representations often expose misconceptions or inaccuracies students have about the new word they are learning. This forces a translation from a linguistic to a nonlinguistic understanding of the word.

Sometimes students, especially those in the early grades, have trouble coming up with nonlinguistic representations. One way to help them is to have them discuss possible images or to provide examples. In the early grades, it may be a matter of students' creating their own personal drawing or symbol that mimics what the teacher drew or presented. Amy Grady, a second-grade teacher, used clip art as a resource for children to create visual representations for words. After discussing the meaning of several words with students, she had them select the picture from clip art files that best represented each word. Then she created a worksheet that had all of the words in a box with clip art representing each word below. Students had to generate sentences that reflected the meaning of the word and place them beside the clip art that represented that word (Figure 4.3).

Figure 4.3.
Visual Representations Using Clip Art

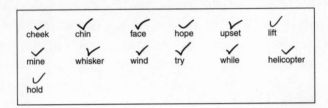

✓	✓	✓	✓	✓	✓
cheek	chin	face	hope	upset	lift
✓	✓	✓	✓	✓	✓
mine	whisker	wind	try	while	helicopter
✓					
hold					

I hope I get a toy.

He is upset.

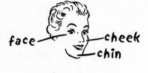

face — cheek — chin

This is my toy.

This crane can lift things.

This man is lifting whates.

I wind up this toy.

In Florida a hurricane has strong wind.

whisker

This girl is holding a bear.

I try to be nice.

I talk while I shop.

A helicopter can lift a person out of the water.

Source: Reprinted by permission of Break-o-Day Elementary School, New Whiteland, Indiana.

Here we look at strategies that students can use in this step:

- Generating mental pictures
- Creating symbols
- Using vocabulary graphic organizers
- Creating kinesthetic representations
- Creating physical models

Strategy: Generating Mental Pictures

Creating mental pictures also asks students to process their understanding into a nonlinguistic form, which helps them determine the degree to which they understand what the word means. Initially you might have students practice creating mental pictures with physical sensations (such as sounds, smells, and emotions) for words they already are familiar with and then have them share their associations with other students. They should come to understand that they do not all have to generate the same mental picture for a word and that several different physical sensations can be attached to that picture. They also should realize that creating mental pictures for a word is a personal experience that relies heavily on their own understanding of the word, background knowledge, and experiences. Adding physical sensations assists them in expanding their mental picture by adding more detail. For example, Ian was trying to remember the word *filament,* so he created a mental picture of his brother, Phil, screwing a lightbulb into a socket. Phil slipped and dropped the bulb and began to lament that he had broken the inside of the lightbulb. While creating his mental picture, he consciously heard the glass break, his mother sigh, and his brother laugh. In addition to this, he placed an expression on Phil's face that showed that he was embarrassed and angry at their reaction. These sounds and emotions helped him put more detail into his mental picture, making it easier for him to retrieve this information later when he needed it.

Students can use mental pictures with physical sensations as a means to remember not only the meaning of the word but also the word itself. In this case, they need to include something in their mental picture to help them remember the word. For example, to remember the word *cur,* students can mentally picture a dog growling. Mentally hearing the "grrrr" sound might remind them of the word.

Students can also record their mental picture as a drawing. Remind them that the pictures they create should help them remember the word and do not have to be artistic creations. In Figure 4.4 a student has created an image to remember the word *rubbish*. In Figure 4.5, students have depicted words associated with a farm.

Strategy: Creating Symbols

When students are asked to create a symbol to represent a word they are learning, it not only stimulates their thinking but also provides a nonlinguistic structure in the mind of the learner that will help him or her remember the word later. Combining this nonlinguistic structure with a student's linguistic representations of the word makes learning more powerful. Since this strategy may be somewhat difficult for young children, it is important that the teacher leads a discussion with

Figure 4.4.
A Student's Drawings of Mental Pictures for the Word *Rubbish*

"rub" bish – you rub it and garbage appears

Source: Reprinted by permission of Jantz Gardner, Iron Horse Elementary School, Parker, Colorado.

students concerning the meaning of the word and helps them generate possible symbols that they might use to represent the word. Young students can select the symbol most meaningful to them, expand or create more detail for that symbol, or if possible, create their own symbol.

Ask students to determine a symbol that conveys the meaning of the new word. This can be a symbol that the student creates or one that may already be used for a particular word. In any case, the symbol is a nonlinguistic representation of what the word means. Again, as with the two previous strategies, tying the linguistic understanding to a nonlinguistic representation helps the student when learning a new word. This symbol should be highly personal, that is, meaningful to the person creating it. Students should be encouraged to share with the other students in the classroom their symbols and why they selected them. While they are doing this, the teacher is free to see if they have any misconceptions about the meaning of the word they are representing. In Figure 4.6, a student has given symbols to some math terms.

Figure 4.5.
Students' Drawings of Mental Pictures of
Words Associated with a Farm

Source: Reprinted by permission of Columbia Elementary School, Har

Figure 4.6.
A Student's Symbols for Math Terms

Source: Reprinted by permission of Columbia Elementary School, Hammond, Indiana.

Strategy: Using Vocabulary Graphic Organizers

The use of a graphic organizer can enable students to uses steps 3 and 4 simultaneously. That is, the visual representation (step 4) is a graphic organizer that is set up in such a way that the explanation, description, examples, and sometimes even nonexamples (all linguistic) from step 3 are placed within the organizer itself. This is a powerful way for students to learn since it links the linguistic representation for a word (description or explanation in words) with a nonlinguistic representation (graphic organizer). There are several different graphic organizers that can be used to organize information about a word.

Descriptive Pattern. A descriptive pattern graphic organizer can be used to represent facts about specific persons, places, things, and events and is very useful for some types of vocabulary terms and phrases (Marzano, Norford, Paynter, Pickering, and Gaddy, 2001).

With a descriptive pattern graphic organizer, the new vocabulary term or phrase or a picture of the term or phrase is written in the center of the graphic organizer. The facts and information related to the new word are written on the outside edges of the graphic organizer (Figure 4.7).

Concept Definition Maps.   The concept definition map (Schwartz, 1988) is a graphic organizer that allows students to identify the word they are learning, a general category this word might be placed in, the essential attributes or characteristics of the word, some examples of the word, and their own definition (Figure 4.8).

Frayer Model.   The Frayer model (Frayer, Frederick, and Klausmeier, 1969) asks students to analyze the attributes or characteristics of a word and identify examples and nonexamples of it. To introduce the use of the Frayer model to students, start with words that are moderately familiar to the students, such as *circus* (Figure 4.9).

Figure 4.7.
A Student's Graphic Organizer for the Word *Penny*

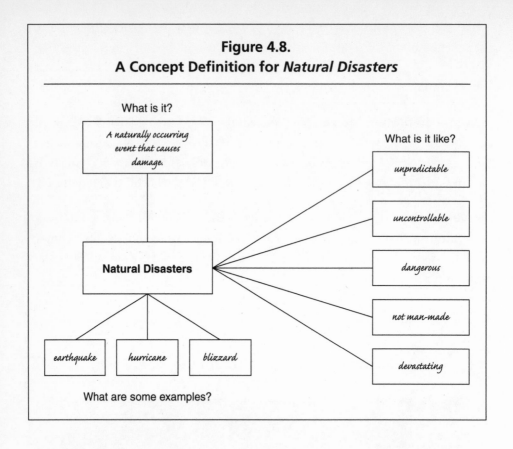

Figure 4.8.
A Concept Definition for *Natural Disasters*

What is it?

A naturally occurring event that causes damage.

What is it like?

unpredictable

uncontrollable

dangerous

not man-made

devastating

Natural Disasters

earthquake   hurricane   blizzard

What are some examples?

This is a good way for children to learn about examples and nonexamples, a relatively abstract notion some students may find difficult. After children have mastered the use of this organizer for defining familiar words, they will be ready to use this strategy for new content vocabulary words such as *crystal* (Figure 4.10).

Strategy: Creating Kinesthetic Representations

It can be very useful to have students engage in physical movement to help them represent the meaning of a term or phrase. Kinesthetic activities help students depict their understanding of the new word and create a "picture" of what they are learning. Not only is this fun for students and helps them release some pent-up energy, but it forces them to process and elaborate on their current understanding of the new word, and, as with creating a symbol for a word, it helps them connect to their linguistic understandings. This can be done in the form of role-play or actual movement.

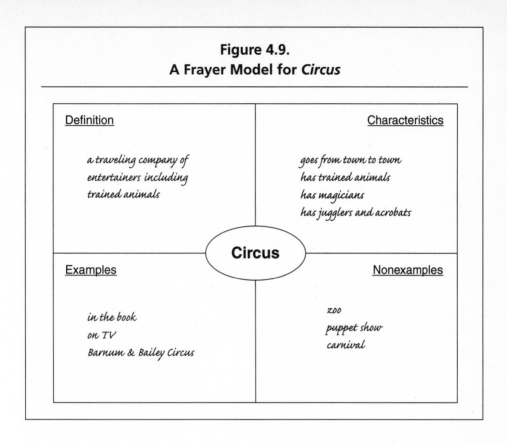

Figure 4.9.
A Frayer Model for *Circus*

Definition

a traveling company of
entertainers including
trained animals

Characteristics

goes from town to town
has trained animals
has magicians
has jugglers and acrobats

Circus

Examples

in the book
on TV
Barnum & Bailey Circus

Nonexamples

zoo
puppet show
carnival

As an example, students in a sixth-grade classroom were learning the following vocabulary that represents the various parts of a tree: *crown, roots, trunk, heartwood, xylem, sapwood, phloem,* and *bark.* Initially the teacher asked each student to create a five- by seven-inch card for each new word. On the front of the card, each student wrote his or her definition of the word and on the back drew a picture or symbol representing that word. Once students completed all of their cards, they were asked to punch a hole and add string to each card. They were then given the directions found in Exhibit 4.2 for creating a kinesthetic representation of the parts of a tree.

Strategy: Creating Physical Models

Physical models are three-dimensional graphic organizers that help students show what they know in a concrete way through representations such as manipulatives and dioramas. We caution you to make sure that the time students are spending on

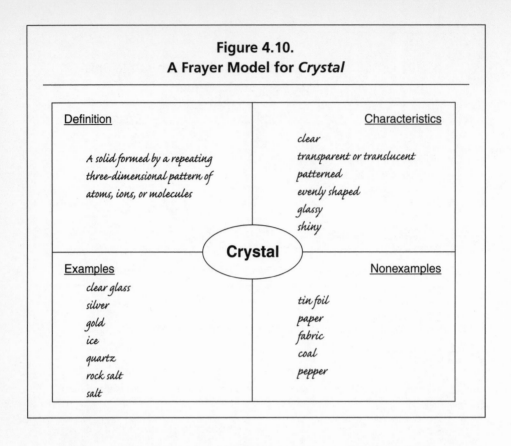

Figure 4.10.
A Frayer Model for *Crystal*

Definition	Characteristics
A solid formed by a repeating three-dimensional pattern of atoms, ions, or molecules	clear transparent or translucent patterned evenly shaped glassy shiny
Examples	**Nonexamples**
clear glass silver gold ice quartz rock salt salt	tin foil paper fabric coal pepper

Crystal

these physical models is not in excess. That is, students can spend inordinate amounts of time creating physical models and the actual learning experience is very minimal. For example, in a science class, the teacher wanted students to understand the difference between *mitosis* and *meiosis*. One of the students decided to create a physical model to depict this difference, and it took her over four hours to complete her model. In addition, she spent fifteen dollars for the materials for her model. Student need to remember that this is not an art project, but rather a simple and quick method of trying to represent a surface level understanding of a new word.

Exhibit 4.2.
Directions for Kinesthetically Representing Words Associated with Trees

Vocabulary: crown, roots, trunk, heartwood, xylem, sapwood, phloem, and bark

Directions:

Place yourself in a group of eight. Have each person in your group select one of the vocabulary words you have been learning. Taking turns, share your word, definition, and symbol or picture and place your card around your neck so that the other students can see the symbol or picture you created.

Once everyone has finished sharing, determine as a group what position each word would take if you were drawing a picture of a tree. Then, rather than drawing that picture, you will be forming a diagram of a tree using your bodies. Discuss how you might do this as a group, and have each person place himself or herself in the correct position on the floor to create the representation of the parts of a tree. For example, if you had the word root, you would share your definition and symbol or picture of a root with the other students and then place yourself on the floor below the person who is representing the word trunk.

Once you have completed forming your representation of a tree, discuss how creating a kinesthetic representation of the parts of a tree helps you remember the new words and their meanings.

STEP 5: STUDENTS DEEPEN THEIR UNDERSTANDING

There are many strategies that students can use to help them extend and refine their understanding of new words. Initially they may have some misconceptions about the new word they are learning. These additional activities help students clear up confusions and misconceptions, make connections with other words they are familiar with, and increase their depth of understanding of the new word.

- Creating analogies

- Creating metaphors

- Completing a semantic feature analysis

- Classifying vocabulary

Strategy: Creating Analogies

When students create analogies for words, they are trying to gain an understanding of the new word by relating it to a term or phrase for which they already have some meaning. In a stricter sense, analogical reasoning is a specific type of thinking in the form *A is to B as C is to D.* For example in the analogy *feather is to bird as leaf is to tree,* the relationship between feather and bird is that of part to whole. To make the analogy correct, the relationship of leaf to tree must also be that of part to whole. We cannot assume that students know how to create analogies and therefore should provide them with a set of steps:

1. Identify how the two elements in the first pair of words are related.

2. State the relationship in a general way.

3. Identify another pair of elements that share a similar relationship (Marzano, Norford, Paynter, Pickering, and Gaddy, 2001).

Model these steps for students and help them understand why creating analogies for new words is an effective strategy for gaining understanding about new terms or phrases. You may even provide them with an explanation, graphic organizer, and the steps for this strategy like the one in Figure 4.11a. Teachers will need to set up worksheets for students to complete their analogies, like the one in Figure 4.11b. In this case, the teacher gave Kay a blank worksheet, and Kay had to create four analogies from the vocabulary words that she was currently learning. Once students have created their analogies, they should be asked to explain and defend the relationships linking the two pairs of words.

Figure 4.11a.

Handout for the Strategy of Creating Analogies (blank)

Strategy: Creating Analogies

This strategy helps you gain a deeper understanding of a new word by relating it to words that you already understand. It involves identifying the relationship between two words you know and then using that relationship to determine another word that has the same relationship with the new word you are learning.

relationship		*relationship*

_____ **:** _____ **as** _____ **:** _____

Steps for creating an analogy:

1. Identify how the two elements in the first pair of words are related.

2. State the relationship in a general way.

3. Identify another pair of elements that share a similar relationship.

Strategy: Creating Metaphors

When we ask students to create vocabulary metaphors, we are asking them to identify how two seemingly different vocabulary terms and phrases are in fact similar. For example, at first glance, it might seem rather difficult to see how a suit is the same as a Teddy Bear, but actually, when you take a step back and look at what they have in common, you can see that both are made of material, both can be bought in a store, and both can be used until they are worn out. As we mentioned in Chapter Two, children have the capacity to understand metaphoric relationships between familiar words or concepts at a very young age. You can build on this capacity to stretch their metaphoric thinking to increasingly abstract concepts. For example, students studying the structure of the cell could be asked to create a metaphor relating to how the cell is like the *Starship Enterprise.* Exercises requiring students to create metaphoric links are among the highest level of cognitive activities that can take place in the classroom (Suhor, 1984).

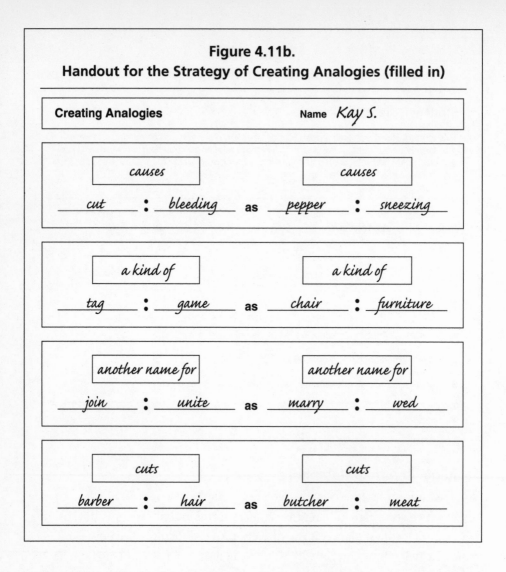

Figure 4.11b.
Handout for the Strategy of Creating Analogies (filled in)

Creating Analogies	Name *Kay S.*

causes   *causes*

___cut___ : ___bleeding___ **as** ___pepper___ : ___sneezing___

a kind of   *a kind of*

___tag___ : ___game___ **as** ___chair___ : ___furniture___

another name for   *another name for*

___join___ : ___unite___ **as** ___marry___ : ___wed___

cuts   *cuts*

___barber___ : ___hair___ **as** ___butcher___ : ___meat___

In order for students to be able to create or complete a vocabulary metaphor, they need to know what the two words will be in the metaphor. They then have to move beyond the specific characteristics or attributes of each word and consider them at a much more general level. By moving to the general level, the relationship between the words can more readily be seen. For example, consider Figure 4.12. The students have been given the metaphor: a political map is a puzzle. The worksheet

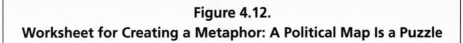

Figure 4.12.
Worksheet for Creating a Metaphor: A Political Map Is a Puzzle

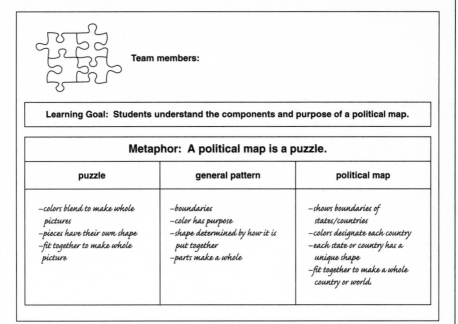

Team members:

Learning Goal: Students understand the components and purpose of a political map.

Metaphor: A political map is a puzzle.

puzzle	general pattern	political map
−colors blend to make whole pictures −pieces have their own shape −fit together to make whole picture	−boundaries −color has purpose −shape determined by how it is put together −parts make a whole	−shows boundaries of states/countries −colors designate each country −each state or country has a unique shape −fit together to make a whole country or world.

is a means to help them figure out the metaphor. First, working in pairs, the students must write down what information they know about a puzzle in the column beneath that word. Next they should write what they know about a political map. Having completed both of these steps, the students are to determine what these two vocabulary terms have in common, and write their thoughts in the middle column. This information then represents the general pattern for these two words.

We cannot assume that students will be able to automatically identify a metaphor or easily recognize a general pattern between two terms or phrases when one is new or unfamiliar. To help them do this, present them with a set of steps, model those steps for students using a think-aloud, and have students practice them using vocabulary terms and phrases that are familiar to them. When students are given two words and asked to explain the general relationship or pattern between these two words, the following process can be used:

1. Identify the attributes or characteristics of the first word in the metaphor.

2. Identify the attributes or characteristics of the second word in the metaphor.

3. Look at the characteristics or attributes for both words of the metaphor and try to find attributes that are somewhat related. State the relationship of these attributes in a very general way by:

   • Replacing words for specific things with words for more general things

   • Summarizing information whenever possible (Marzano, Norford, Paynter, Pickering, and Gaddy, 2001)

A variation of these steps is used when the goal is for students to identify a new word around which a metaphor could be created:

1. Identify the attributes or characteristics of the new word that you are learning.

2. Write those attributes or characteristics in a more general pattern by:

   • Replacing words for specific things with words for more general things

   • Summarizing information whenever possible

3. Identify a second word that follows the same general pattern and that would complete the metaphor.

In the worksheet in Figure 4.13, students were given the term *developed country* and were asked to identify another word or word that represented a metaphor. Working in teams of three, the students identified the attributes or what they knew about a developed country and placed this information in the first column. Using the first column as their guide, they translated each statement in the first column into a more general statement and placed it in the middle column. They did this until they had addressed all of the statements from the first column. Then they read all the information in the middle column and tried to think of a new term or word that had the same general pattern. They determined that they thought that a businessperson was the same as a developed country because they both followed this same general pattern. In column 3, students then wrote down the specific ways in which a businessperson met the statements found in the general pattern in the middle column.

Figure 4.13.
Worksheet for Creating a Metaphor:
"Developed Country" and "Businessperson"

developed country		
attributes of word	general pattern	new word businessperson
−high literacy rate −low birth rate −low death rate −lots of industry −good infrastructure −high GNP	−good education −good standard of living −good production −strong support system −well-developed economy	−college degree −comfortable lifestyle −good production −leadership −generates money

As children are learning to use this organizer to analyze metaphors, we suggest starting with examples of simple concrete metaphors that they know, such as comparing clouds to pillows (both are white, soft, and fluffy). After children have had some experience using organizers and develop a better understanding of how metaphors are created, they can apply this skill to more abstract terms. For example they can analyze the metaphor that *nutrients* are the *building blocks* of our body.

Strategy: Completing a Semantic Feature Analysis

The semantic feature analysis strategy (Johnson and Pearson, 1984) helps students determine a word's meaning by comparing words that are semantically related. To do this, students are given a matrix that contains a number of key vocabulary terms or phrases that are semantically related, along with a list of several characteristics or features related to the category that these terms and phrases would belong in. They place the key terms or phrases along the left side of the matrix and write the characteristics or features they are comparing along the top of the matrix. Students then think about the word and determine whether to place an X in the box for each characteristic or feature for each term or phrase (Figure 4.14).

Figure 4.14.
Student Worksheet for Semantic Feature Analysis

Semantic Feature Analysis

Category or feature	Wings	Fins	Legs	Feathers	Hair/Fur	Scales
Koala Bear 			X		X	
Rattlesnake 						X
Platypus 			X		X	
Snowy Owl 	X		X	X		
Shark 		X			X	
Chameleon 			X		X	
Mouse 			X		X	

This strategy is somewhat difficult for younger children because they usually are not given an entire group of new vocabulary terms at a time. This strategy could be used to help primary students develop a deeper understanding of more abstract terms like *transportation* that they have a cursory understanding of but do not know their exact meaning. For example, they could be given a worksheet with various forms of transportation shown in the first column (such as a bike, car, plane, river, and stroller) and then given the categories to consider: "takes you places," "is man-made," "does not move by itself," and "uses fuel." When using this strategy with younger children, we suggest that students be allowed to work in small groups or complete the analysis as a whole group.

Strategy: Classifying Vocabulary

Asking students to create categories or classify words helps them think of the distinctions among words that might be similar in meaning. Often they might initially classify them in obvious categories. Moving them beyond the obvious helps them see finer distinctions and deepens their understanding of the words they are classifying. For example, students might be learning about the characteristics of mammals, birds, amphibians, and reptiles. Initially the teacher might give students the task of classifying twenty different animals into these categories. In this classification task, there can be only one correct answer. That is, all of the children, if they were to complete the worksheet correctly, would have the same answer. If the teacher then asked students to reclassify the animals looking at the various characteristics they possessed rather than the previous categories, students would be able to learn more about these items. In other words, they would not have to classify them as mammals, birds, amphibians, and reptiles, but rather would have to focus on each animal separately and examine its characteristics. When they have finished this task, students might have different answers, depending on the characteristics they focused on. The accountability for the answers being correct lies in how each category is defined by the student and if the animal has that characteristic. This reclassifying task helps the student think about the items they are classifying in different ways, moving beyond what would be the most obvious classification.

STEP 6: STUDENTS ENGAGE IN VOCABULARY GAMES AND WORD PLAY

This last step engages students in additional experiences that help them remember the new word and its meaning. Playing with words can be fun and interesting to children, especially when they are trying to create a specific effect when communicating with others. These humorous interactions with words require students to explore and experiment with language. They come in many forms: idioms, proverbs, oxymorons, homographs, homophones, anagrams, alliterations, riddles, slogans, and tongue twisters, among others. We have included examples of some word games here assuming that you will use them as a way of extending students' experiences with words you have already taught through direct instruction.

Word Game: Match Me

Mr. Waters wants to help his kindergartners learn the words for everyday objects, such as *planter, sharpener, frame, globe, dictionary, cardigan, action figure/figurine, domino,* and *keyhole.* so he makes word cards for those items. He divides the class into two groups, and each child in one group is given a word and told to find and hold it or point to it. Then he mixes up the word cards for those items and distributes them randomly to the other group of children. The children with the word cards then have to find the classmate who is holding or pointing to the object. For additional exposures to the same group of words, Mr. Waters often times how long it takes the children to match words to items on one day and then several days later challenges the class to beat their previous time.

Word Game: Colorful Songs

Ms. Mayer looks for songs that use engaging and interesting language. When children are learning color words, she has them sit them on the floor in a circle with colored construction paper pieces that represent the primary colors. She then sings songs about the different colors. The children hold up the piece of paper that matches the color as Ms. Mayer sings the color word. A smile and a nod let the children know they have the correct color.

Word Game: Cluster Beanbag

The children sit in a circle in Ms. Sandvik's second-grade class, ready to pass a beanbag around. She selects a category, such as "things related to flying," tells the children what the category is, and then says a word that relates to that category. If the word she says describes something that flies, such as *wings* or *helicopter,* the child who is holding the beanbag keeps it. If the word does not describe something that flies, such as *snake* or *subway,* the child passes the beanbag to his or her neighbor.

Word Game: Vocabulary Bingo

Ms. Singh has a master list of words her students are expected to learn that year and makes a set of word cards from the list. As she introduces each word, each member of the class writes their own definition for it. The student-generated definitions and, when appropriate, symbols or illustrations, are recorded on a second set of cards (which use a different color paper from the initial set). She uses these cards to play Vocabulary Bingo.

For Vocabulary Bingo, Ms. Singh gives each student a blank four- by four-inch or five- by five-inch bingo card and has a volunteer read the vocabulary words from a set of word cards. Students write each word in a blank space of their choosing on their game boards, so every student's game board is different from the others (Figure 4.15). When all players have completed their game boards, Vocabulary Bingo

Figure 4.15.
Vocabulary Bingo Card

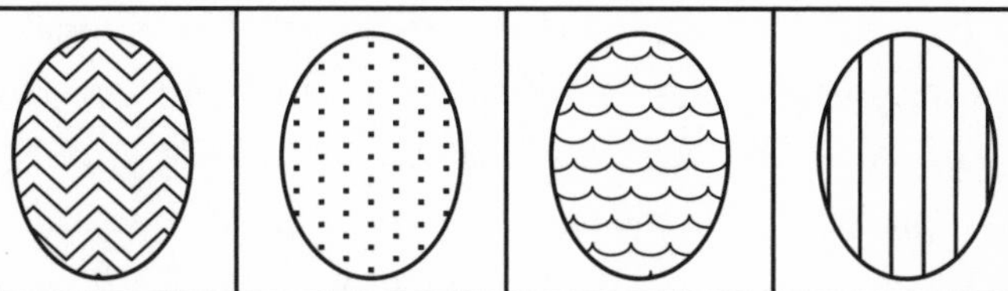

hopped	colorful	parade	April
jellybean	dye	rabbit	spray
basket	Easter	hunt	talk
hopping	bonnet	green	sunflower
design	boiled	plants	rose

Source: Reprinted by permission of Columbia Elementary School, Hammond, Indiana.

begins. A student caller reads the definition cards aloud, one at a time. Players mark their game board spaces when they hear the definition. The winner is the first player to mark four or five words in a row horizontally, vertically, or diagonally. The caller checks the words on the player's game board to see that they match the definition cards read. For added variety, Ms. Singh changes the rules for winning; for example, words must form the letter L or T, a zigzag pattern across the game board, or be in the four corners.

Word Game: Pass the Right Word

Mr. Frost wants to give his fourth-graders additional experiences with the words they are learning, so he plays a game with them that he calls Pass the Right Word. Since he has a variety of word clusters scattered around his room, he uses these as the basis for his game. He takes ten words from a cluster and writes each one on a small white card. All of the cards from that cluster are then placed in a pile, and a rubber band is placed around the pile. When he is finished with all of the clusters on the wall, he has about twenty stacks of cards in clusters.

The students then are placed on two teams: Team A and Team B. A pair of students from each team comes to the front of the room, and one of the players (player 1) from each team is given a stack of cards. The pair from Team A goes first. Player 1 tells his or her partner (player 2) the name of the cluster of words—for example, types of machines. Player 1 then takes each card one at a time and presents other words that are similar in meaning to the word on the card to player 2 to act as clues to what the word is on the card—for example, *lever, pulley, screw, wedge, axel*. If player 2 cannot guess the word, player 1 can move on to the next word. Typically the team is given a time limit to complete all ten words in their stack of cards. They then record the number of words player 2 answered correctly.

When this is finished, the pair from Team B has its turn. Mr. Frost allows several pairs of players to compete in this game depending on how much time is available.

Word Game: Vocabulary Scramble

Ms. Gonzales, who teaches fifth grade, decided to take the words on her vocabulary list and place them in semantically related clusters. Luckily, she could do this by just cutting and pasting her original list on the computer. She then printed off several different clusters. To try to keep track of the words in the cluster, she took a small envelope and wrote the name of the cluster on the envelope. She then took the words for each cluster, cut them into little strips, and placed them in the envelope. When she was done, she had about twenty envelopes.

Now she was ready to have her students play Vocabulary Scramble. She divided her classroom into two teams: Team A and Team B. Then she took out a small bowl and emptied the contents of two of the envelopes into the bowl. A pair of students from each team was asked to come to the front of the room. The goal of the game was for each pair to get their team to say as many of the words in the bowl as possible within a specified time limit (usually one minute). The pair selected a word from the bowl and gave similar words as cues to the members of their team, who could call out what they thought the word was. If they called out the right word, the pair could then go on to another word. If they picked up a word and did not know its meaning, they could place it back in the bowl and pick up another word. When the time limit was up, they added up the number of words their team members had identified and wrote their score on the board. The same process was repeated for Team B. Several rounds of the game gave students a quick review of the essential vocabulary for their grade level.

Word Game: Pyramid Clusters

Every Friday, Mr. Garcia's sixth-grade classroom is alive with vocabulary games. His students' favorite is Pyramid Clusters. He creates a pyramid on the chalkboard divided into several compartments. His students are divided into two teams: Team A and Team B. A pair of students from Team A comes to the front of the classroom and places their backs to the chalkboard. He then writes in the names of various clusters within the compartments of the pyramid, along with the number of points assigned to each compartment (Figure 4.16). The members of Team A who are sitting at their desks have a designated amount of time (usually about one or two minutes) to have the pair at the front of the classroom name the clusters. Mr. Garcia points to the first cluster, and the team members shout out words that belong in that cluster. When the pair up front guesses the cluster heading, the teacher points to the next cluster, and so on until either the time is up or Team A has completed all of the clusters in the pyramid. Team A then adds up and records its score. Mr. Garcia now creates another pyramid with clusters for Team B to play. Students usually have time to play several rounds of this game.

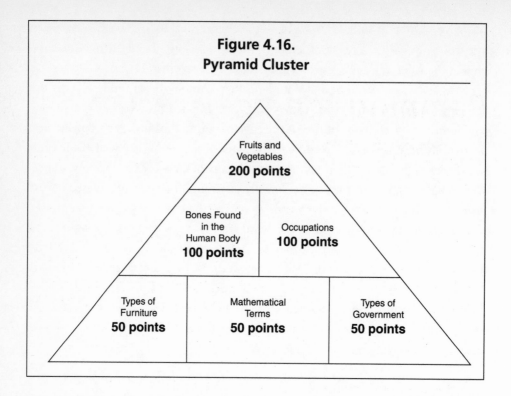

Figure 4.16.
Pyramid Cluster

Fruits and Vegetables
200 points

Bones Found in the Human Body
100 points

Occupations
100 points

Types of Furniture
50 points

Mathematical Terms
50 points

Types of Government
50 points

SUMMARY

In this chapter, we have set out a six-step process for teaching vocabulary using direct instruction. In addition, we have shared examples of multiple vocabulary learning strategies and some vocabulary games. As you consider how to plan direct instruction experiences, determine which of the strategies you would like your students to learn. Remember that it is important for you to model these strategies, have children apply them to words they are familiar with, and then apply them to the new words they are learning. Giving students feedback on how they are doing will help them become proficient in using the strategies. The goal is that over time, your students will become very independent in using these strategies.

In the next chapter, we focus on planning incidental learning experiences for your students.

Planning for Incidental Learning

In Chapter Three, we introduced the concept of planned incidental learning experiences. To create the conditions for these learning experiences, we recommend the following practices:

- Create a vocabulary-rich classroom environment.
- Create semantic cluster walls that promote incidental learning and act as a record of the new words students are learning.
- Expand students' wide reading experiences.
- Carefully select read-aloud experiences to expand students' vocabulary.

CREATE A VOCABULARY-RICH ENVIRONMENT

Children need to be surrounded by new words, both orally and through written text. There are multiple ways that this can happen. We suggest the following strategies:

- Place vocabulary purposefully around the classroom.
- Select books and resources that enhance vocabulary learning.
- Use a robust vocabulary with students, and hold them accountable for learning and using those words.

Strategy: Place Vocabulary Purposefully Around the Classroom

If you looked around your classroom right now, what would you see? Is it a place where children are constantly exposed to new words, or is it a rather barren wasteland for vocabulary growth? If you want students to learn new words, they need to be surrounded by them. The following are activities you might use to place vocabulary more purposefully around your classroom.

All for Labels and Labels for All!   Mr. Thiess labels everything and therefore fills his first-grade classroom with words. When students understand all the words he has around the classroom when they hear them, he adds more. To the *armchair* label in the reading corner, he adds the word *comfortable.* When children notice the new label, he takes a few minutes to discuss it and list all the different kinds of chairs they are familiar with. He has students compare how comfortable the chairs in the reading corner are to those at their desks.

He likes to keep labeling activities fresh, so occasionally he mixes the labels up and asks his students to tell him where the proper ones belong. For example, he puts the *chalkboard* label on the bulletin board and the *library corner* label in the art area. Just before Halloween, he tells the children that he thought he saw a very small ghost (or goblin, gremlin, elf, leprechaun, or fairy) fly out of the window just as he walked in. He's not sure if the ghost did any mischief, but if they see anything that is not quite right, they need to help fix it. Mr. Thiess ties his mischief-makers to holidays, special events, or books he is reading to the class. Then he praises the group for restoring the labels to their proper places.

Ms. Quackenboss, a fifth-grade teacher, sees how Mr. Thiess uses labeling in his classroom and decides that she can use more sophisticated labels in her classroom, such as labeling the light switch the *electrical circuit connector* and a window the *transparent sunlight emitter.* She also challenges her students to create their own labels for items around the room and selects upcoming content-area vocabulary words and places them around the room as "mystery words." Sometimes she includes nonlinguistic representations, such as a symbol, icon, or picture, with each new word and then asks students to see if they can figure out the meaning of the word from the representation (Figure 5.1).

Ms. Quackenboss also likes to introduce the word *detective* and the concept of a *red herring.* This tactic helps her students who rely heavily on context clues to

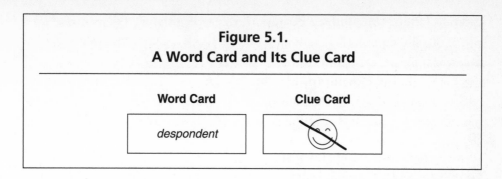

Figure 5.1.
A Word Card and Its Clue Card

Word Card

| despondent |

Clue Card

work a little harder to find the true meaning of a word. She warns students that some of the clues surrounding new words may be confusing rather than helpful, and so she asks her "detectives" to devise strategies for figuring out what the new words mean.

Field Trip Follow-Up.   Every year, Ms. Navarro takes her kindergarten class to a train station and photographs the people they meet there and the things they see. Back in the classroom, she labels the photographs—*engineer, conductor, timetable, arrival,* and *departure,* for example—and places them in the dramatic play center, where the children use the words when they play "train station." For example, as they write numbers on pretend tickets, they talk of it as a "seat assignment," and when the teacher asks why Vincent is lying on two chairs, other children explain that he is in a "sleeping car."

Vocabulary Preview.   Ms. Przywara creates a list of vocabulary words to teach her fifth-grade class. (See Chapter Six for more information about creating your own word list.) She determines which of these words she will focus on each quarter, based on the lessons and units that she will teach. At the beginning of the quarter, she places several labeled items around the room representing the words children will be learning. These words serve as teasers. The children who know the words are happy to share what they mean with their classmates and to supply nonlinguistic representations to show other students what the words mean. Ms. Przywara makes a special point of praising their knowledge. The positive reinforcement encourages the whole class to learn other new words.

Words of Interest.   Ms. Donis wants to create an environment in which her class will notice and be excited by new words. She makes a space on her walls to record new words the children come across and find interesting. Next to the word, children give her an explanation of what the word means. Then they draw a picture to help others understand the meaning of the word, and the words, their meanings, and pictures are on display for all to see. Ms. Donis makes time for children to share their words and pictures with the whole class.

Looking Up Words.   Ms. Wheatley uses the ceiling in her classroom as a huge mobile. She selects interesting and intriguing words, writes them on large cards attached to strings, and hangs them from the ceiling. As students learn the meaning of these new words, they can hang their own cards where they have written what that word means in their own words and have created a simple drawing or symbol depicting that meaning.

Word Wise.   Ms. Block dedicates a bulletin board to help students understand that words are important. She asks her students to describe on index cards situations they have encountered when they were confused and did not know what to do because they did not know the meaning of a word. Students share their situations with others and then place their cards on the bulletin board. For example, on her first card, one student wrote, "The coach said she did not need so many onlookers," followed by her confusion: "I did not know where to look." During a class discussion, the teacher pulled the card, read what was on it, and then the class discussed why this was confusing and what *onlooker* really meant. Another student wrote on his card, "Since there was no unanimous decision, we could not finish the project." During the following discussion with the teacher, the class concluded that this student had confused *unanimous* with *anonymous*. He was confused because the teacher said the class needed to reach a unanimous decision on how to proceed with the project, but he wanted his name on it.

Meet-and-Greet.   Ms. Searson sets aside time during class meetings to "meet-and-greet" new vocabulary words. She selects words from books she is reading aloud to her class, words students will be learning in content areas, words from current events, and words relevant to her community—both her neighborhood and her town. She writes the words on large index cards, keeps them in a basket, and encourages students to find interesting words to add to the basket. She then has a volunteer select a card at random from the basket and asks the class if they know what it means. If they are correct, she praises them and adds to their explanation. If they do not know the word, she gives clues or asks questions to help. Then she asks students to think of situations in which they might use the word and records their ideas on the back of the word cards that are kept in the basket for students to investigate during independent reading. She also encourages students to use the word cards for story writing and word games.

Strategy: Select Books and Resources That Enhance Vocabulary Learning

Choose books and reading resources on topics that interest children at different reading levels for the classroom library. Look for materials that introduce colorful and interesting words. Students also need tools and resources for finding the meaning of new words, including dictionaries and thesauruses. The following are activities you can use to enhance vocabulary learning.

Book Baskets.   For each new theme Ms. Gibbs introduces to her kindergarten class, she creates a book basket, grouping books by theme or category. Each book basket is labeled according to the category—animals, community helpers, transportation, and so on. Children use the book baskets during independent reading time. In addition to reading practice, children learn that words can be grouped into larger categories. For example, books about boats, helicopters, and trains are all in the "transportation" book basket.

Disaster Dictionary.   As part of a unit on weather, Mr. Sposili's class creates a "Disaster Dictionary." For each word, students draw two pictures. One picture shows the natural disaster, such as a hurricane, earthquake, or monsoon, and how it looks. The second picture illustrates what people should (or should not) do to be safe.

Reasonable Resources.   The good news: Mr. Mickens has a class set of dictionaries. The problem: the dictionaries are all the same, they are too hard for some students, and the definitions are complex and do not provide rich explanations or context sentences to help students make meaning.

Mr. Mickens decides to write a small grant proposal to purchase a variety of dictionaries for his classroom. With the grant money, he also plans to buy several different types of thesauruses for students to use. This is important because students have various levels of word understanding and need resources that assist them at their own level.

Non-Webster Dictionaries.   At the beginning of each school year, Ms. Poole gives her class a list of the essential vocabulary words they will learn that year. Monthly, she divides the class into groups to have them create their own "non-Webster" dictionaries for some of the words. Students write their own definitions and explanations of the words and add a drawing, symbol, or icon to represent each word. The dictionaries have a special place in the reference section of the classroom library.

Strategy: Use a Robust Vocabulary with Children and Expect Them to Learn New Words

Many teachers, especially in the younger grades, use words that they are sure children will understand rather than words that will move them beyond their current vocabulary. When you expose children to new words, you create an interest, a curiosity, and an appreciation for vocabulary learning. There are many opportunities every day to employ an expanded, robust vocabulary. Try some of these activities.

Sophisticated Synonyms.   Using familiar words in different contexts helps students understand the small but significant differences in words that have similar meanings. For example, the words *clothes, costume, dress, outfit, garment, garb,* and *uniform* have close meanings and can describe the same piece of clothing. It is said that these words are close in their *connotation.* However, these words have different nuances in meaning and cannot be used interchangeably in all cases. For example, ask children which of these words they would use in the sentences in Exhibit 5.1. Also ask them why these words would be appropriate and others would not.

Children should come to learn the subtleties of the differences in what words mean through the various contexts that they encounter. The words *smug, vain, haughty,* and *arrogant* all have the same general meaning, but each word has small distinctions that provide additional insight into the character of a person:

A *smug* person can be self-righteous but not necessarily vain.

A *vain* person can be conceited but not condescending.

A *haughty* person can be condescending but not self-righteous.

An *arrogant* person can be full of self-importance but not vain.

Exhibit 5.1.
Sample Sentences for Choosing the Right Word

Complete the sentences by choosing the correct word from the following:

clothes	costume	dress	uniforms

outfit   garment   garb

The soldiers were wearing old khaki _____ covered with dust.

At the New Year's Eve party, Chris won the first prize for best _____ .

Clarissa looked nice in her pretty summer _____ .

All four words—*smug, vain, haughty* and *arrogant*—make us think of an individual who has a lot of pride. However, each of these words describes the individual more accurately and helps us to have a deeper understanding of that person.

In using new words in the classroom and pointing out subtle distinctions, you can create an environment that invites children to think about words. They will realize what a powerful feeling it is to choose the exact word for a given situation.

For example, whenever Mr. Pope reads aloud to students, he points out one or more new words that he thinks are interesting. Then he asks students if they know any other words that have similar meanings. He spends a few minutes talking about the distinctions among these words and, when appropriate, has the students act them out.

Once Mr. Pope used this example from *The House of Dies Drear* (Hamilton, 1968, p. 38): "He opened one of the doors off the hall, paused, and then beckoned them to come." He chose the word *beckoned.* Students offered these synonyms: *gestured, signaled,* and *motioned.* Mr. Pope then encouraged the class to suggest situations and sentences for using the new word and its synonyms.

Master of Disguises.   Reading a book to her kindergarten class, Ms. Evanovich paused after the word *disguise* and asked children what they thought this word meant. Children came up with an example when they would wear a disguise (Halloween) and with another word that would describe what they are doing when they are wearing a disguise—*dressing up.* From this day on, Ms. Evanovich started referring to the dress-up clothes in the dramatic play area as "disguises," which the children thought was very funny.

Face It.   Try introducing more complex vocabulary for words students are currently using. For example, when children return from physical education class, say, "You look rather parched. You could probably use a drink of water." Students can deduce that *parched* is a synonym for *thirsty.* Having a conversation about it will help reinforce the word in students' minds.

When Mr. McIlroy's students return to the classroom from recess, he greets them with vocabulary words that describe the child's expression or physical state. He has a brief conversation with each child, such as the one below, guiding them to use the new word:

> *Mr. McIlroy:* Hilary, you look *flushed.* Your face is red, and you're out of breath.
> *Hilary:* [looking in a mirror] My face is red! I look *flushed!*
> [Jesse comes in with dirt all over his jeans and a scratch down his arm.]
> *Mr. McIlroy:* And Jesse looks *disheveled.*
> *Jesse:* What does *disheveled* mean?
> *Mr. McIlroy: Disheveled* means your clothes and hair look very messy and untidy.
> *Jesse:* [looks down at his shirt tails and untied shoelaces] I never heard that word before. I like it! Look at me! I'm *disheveled!*

CREATE SEMANTIC CLUSTER WALLS

Semantic cluster walls are bulletin boards of words that are organized according to semantic relationships—that is, words with important characteristics in common are clustered together. The clusters contain some words the students know and some new words. Words can even be categorized within clusters to form mini-clusters, which help students reflect on subtle differences among the words in the cluster (Figure 5.2).

Semantic clusters make it easier to learn new words because they are presented within a context. That is, the title of the cluster and some of the words in that cluster provide a context that brings meaning to the unknown words found there. For example, the *words teepee, hogan, igloo, tent,* and *wikiup* could all be grouped into

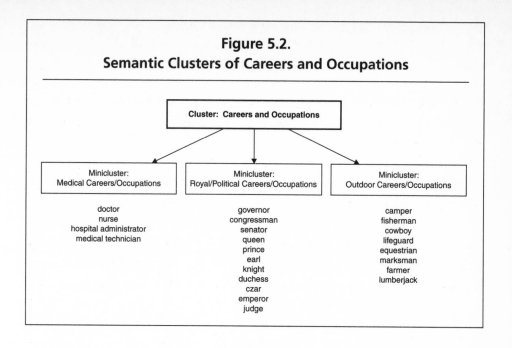

Figure 5.2.
Semantic Clusters of Careers and Occupations

Cluster: Careers and Occupations

Minicluster: Medical Careers/Occupations	Minicluster: Royal/Political Careers/Occupations	Minicluster: Outdoor Careers/Occupations
doctor	governor	camper
nurse	congressman	fisherman
hospital administrator	senator	cowboy
medical technician	queen	lifeguard
	prince	equestrian
	earl	marksman
	knight	farmer
	duchess	lumberjack
	czar	
	emperor	
	judge	

a cluster called "Places People Live." If students did not know the meaning of *hogan*, they would be able to glean from the cluster that it is a place to live in. In addition, they may have some understanding that Native American populations typically have been associated with many of the other words in the cluster, and so they might assume that a *hogan* is a place to live that might be associated with Native American populations. And although these places to live may not be structures students have actually seen or experienced, they can predict that people from other places or other times would live there. Adding a picture or drawing next to each word also helps students construct meaning for the new word.

Semantic clusters help students use their prior knowledge to determine what a new word means, make connections among words, and clear up confusions that they might have about words. For example, in a first-grade classroom, students were talking about trees and grasses. One student had recently been on a trip where he had seen bamboo growing and wanted to add that word to the semantic cluster "plants," but more specifically in a minicluster called "trees." The teacher then explained to students that although bamboo looked like a tree, it was actually a grass, and they would have to put the word in the minicluster that included grasses.

Creating a semantic cluster wall can help students develop a more flexible understanding of words by addressing multiple meanings and subtle differences or nuances. The wall provides a venue for discussion and a context that leads to increased clarity of words with similar meanings. Semantic clusters can also help students see categorical relationships and links among words, as well as distinctions among words that are similar. This increased understanding helps bridge the gap between reading fluency and comprehension. It allows students to better interpret the meaning of the text they are reading and provides a way for creating a full range of contexts for vocabulary learning that would not be possible through direct instruction. In addition, the cluster wall can be used as a basis for spelling and writing.

Cluster walls are living, growing records of increased vocabulary learning for the classroom as a whole because the students and the teacher are constantly adding new words to the wall to keep it alive. Encourage students to create pictorial representations of the words or symbols to represent the words, and the cluster walls become even more vibrant.

The words on the wall can represent the vocabulary for direct and planned incidental experiences and can also be taken from students' random vocabulary experiences. Cluster walls can be used across disciplines and provide multiple exposures to individual words as students revisit clusters, talk about differences among words, and use words from the clusters for their writing. They offer students a resource for words by creating a personal class thesaurus around content they are currently learning, such as the math cluster found in Figure 5.3. As students learn these words, they have easy access to them through the cluster wall.

EXPAND STUDENTS' WIDE READING EXPERIENCES

Some students have parents who are able to take them places and provide experiences that help build their background knowledge. This background knowledge is useful as it can help students interpret new experiences they encounter. Other students may not have these opportunities. Although it would be beneficial, schools cannot be expected to take students out into the world on field trips so that all will have the same and equal number of learning opportunities to build their background knowledge and experiences. Nevertheless, schools can create opportunities for students to view certain experiences through reading. Reading can provide

Figure 5.3.
A Cluster Wall for Math Vocabulary

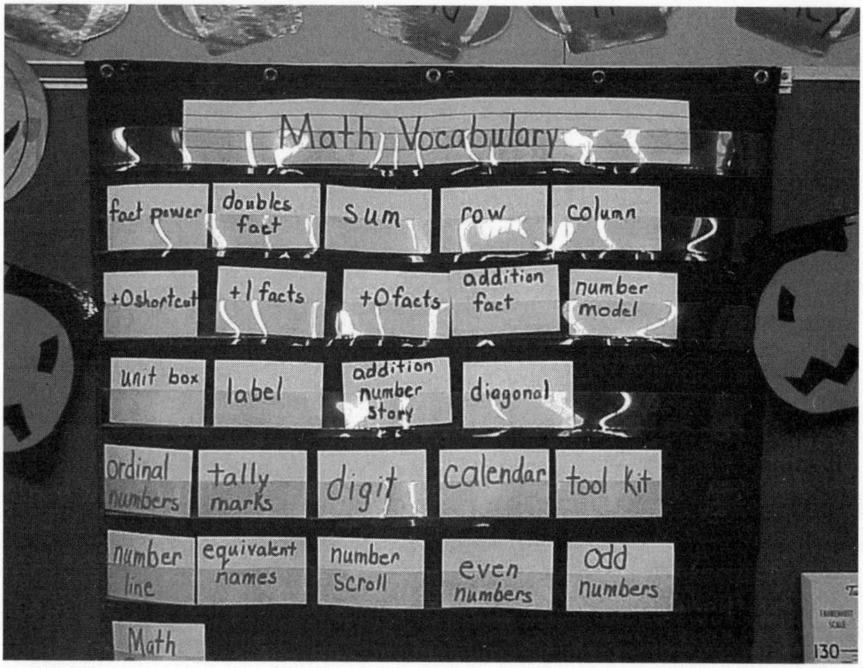

students a virtual window to the world, offering through the written text that which they could not experience directly (Marzano, 2004).

One way to help increase students' background knowledge is to engage them in wide reading experiences that create virtual experiences related to your vocabulary lists. In other words, thoughtfully select materials for wide reading based on words that students need to be learning—books that provide multiple encounters with essential words. Students can be encouraged to keep a record of interesting and intriguing words that they come across during their wide reading experiences and to learn the meaning of these words and share them with their classmates. It is also important to carve out time for students to have discussions around the books that they are reading and to share these experiences with one another.

CAREFULLY SELECT READ-ALOUD EXPERIENCES TO EXPAND STUDENTS' VOCABULARY

Read-alouds can be an important vehicle for vocabulary growth because they expose students to unfamiliar words in an unthreatening environment. Teachers should thoughtfully select books for reading aloud, keeping in mind the vocabulary students need to learn.

There are times when paying too much attention to the pictures, at the expense of text, can get in the way of learning new vocabulary words. For example, when young children look at a picture, they can already describe what they see with words they know. If they see a picture of someone angry, they will not necessarily pay attention to the word *frustrated* if it is in the text. Encourage students to listen and see pictures in their mind as you read aloud. Then show the pictures when the story is read.

Before reading aloud to students, you may wish to point out words you want them to focus on as they listen. At the end of the story, ask students to describe what they thought the words meant. After the students have had the opportunity to review the words with you, show the pictures and reread the sentences containing the new vocabulary words.

For upper elementary students, have them create a section in a notebook to jot down words they hear that they like while they listen during a read-aloud experience. Students could also have sections for different parts of speech, where they might jot down interesting adverbs or adjectives. When you have finished reading, students can raise their hands to list the words they have identified, and as a class, you can discuss the meanings and how they are used. This process is less disruptive than stopping in the middle of a reading to answer students' questions, which can break the flow and impede comprehension.

SUMMARY

Systematically planning for incidental learning experiences can make a big difference in the number of words that students learn throughout the school year. These experiences do not have to take a lot of time and can be part of the everyday context of the classroom. Incidental learning experiences also contribute to students' enjoyment of learning and using new words.

Which words should you use to plan both the direct instruction and incidental learning experiences for your students? In Chapter Six, we explore creating a customized vocabulary list.

Creating a Customized Word List

A t this point, you might be wondering, *How do I decide what words students should be learning in school?* Many teachers struggle with this question. They know that vocabulary is important, yet they are unsure as to what criteria to use to identify the essential vocabulary for their students. They want to bridge the vocabulary gap but are overwhelmed by all of the lists from all of the resources: textbooks, basal readers, and off-the-shelf vocabulary programs, among others. They realize that they could never teach students all of the words on these lists. And they remain unconvinced that these lists contain the words that will be most relevant and meaningful to their particular students. Consider the dilemma that two teachers might face:

Kelly Marchbanks, a fourth-grade teacher in Florida, is sitting at her desk trying to plan the teaching and learning activities for her students. Given all the demands that are placed on her and her students, she realizes that she must be careful in making decisions regarding what her students should be learning in her classroom.

In previewing the student data she has been collecting, she realizes that many of her students are deficient in vocabulary and that this is having a tremendous effect on their ability to understand new content. In reflecting on her practices, she knows that she needs to spend more time helping her low-performing students learn more words, but she is frustrated as she tries to determine which words will provide the foundation they will need to be successful not only in fourth-grade content but in the grades to come.

On her desk is a stack of textbooks that identify vocabulary lists for each of the subject areas. As she reviews these lists, she decides to take a deeper look at her state and district standards and benchmarks. Although the textbooks provide good information, they are not as closely aligned with the state standards and benchmarks as they need to be. Suddenly the task of determining what vocabulary her students should be learning seems overwhelming.

In a classroom in Wyoming, Gordon Cottrell, a kindergarten teacher, is struggling with similar issues. He is aware that some of his students have come to school with a much more robust vocabulary than others. As he contemplates teaching and learning activities for his students, he is concerned that the vocabulary of some of his students is so limited that it will be a stumbling block for their building essential literacy skills.

He has been given several lists of words, such as the Dolch list and other high-frequency words, but he realizes that these lists contain sight words, that is, words students should be able to read, rather than words needed to develop a robust vocabulary. As he considers the books he will be using with his students, he knows they contain many words that students do not know, yet all of these unknown words do not seem to have equal importance. He understands that vocabulary learning is more than just learning vast numbers of words; the words students should learn in kindergarten should be a foundation for building capacity in reading. He also knows that the context in which the word is presented plays an essential role that allows students to make connections among words.

Mr. Cottrell is not sure which words should be the focus of vocabulary learning for his kindergarten students and is concerned that there are so many words and lists and so little time allocated for students to learn these words.

WHY CREATE A CUSTOMIZED VOCABULARY LIST?

We suspect that you find yourself in a dilemma similar to one of these two teachers. This chapter is designed to provide you with resources and support for creating your own customized vocabulary list. In the previous chapters, you have learned that while children are still at home, there is a strong need for vocabulary that relates to their everyday lives. As they enter and progress through elementary school, there is increased need for a more content-based and increasingly more complex and abstract vocabulary. In addition, there are words students need to know to build a strong base for reading that may not necessarily be considered content-area vocabulary. Although many children enter school knowing many of these commonly used words, some children are behind in this area. In addition, as students engage in reading and assessment experiences in school, there may be vocabulary they will need that is not typically associated with the subject-area content they will be learning. As a teacher, you need to consider all of these various sources as you create your customized list, but keep in mind that it is the *content-area vocabulary that will build the strongest foundation for academic achievement.*

RESOURCES FOR CREATING A CUSTOMIZED LIST

To create your customized list, we suggest the following resources:

- The state and district standards and benchmarks documents for the grade level you are teaching. You may also find it helpful to have a copy of the benchmarks that precede and follow the grade level you are teaching.

- A list of basic vocabulary words for the grade level you teach. The lists for grades K–6 are in the Appendix of this book.

- The fiction and nonfiction books students will encounter as part of their language arts experiences.

- Any other resources that identify words students need to learn for the district, state, and national assessments they will be taking.

   In the rest of this section, we present our rationale for using these resources and then set out a four-part process for creating your own customized vocabulary list using these resources.

State and District Standards and Benchmarks Documents

Each state has standards and benchmarks that set out the knowledge and skills that students are supposed to learn. Over the past several years, increasing emphasis has been placed on collecting evidence about whether students are meeting the expected levels of proficiency for the standards and benchmarks.

At the elementary school level, most state standards documents articulate the benchmarks within the content areas of math, science, social studies, language arts, health, and some others. Many states have benchmarks for each grade level, and others have identified the benchmarks as grade spans (for example, for grades 3 through 5). In states with grade spans, the districts or individual schools typically determine which benchmark is most appropriate for which grade level.

Given the emphasis on state and local standards and benchmarks, it makes sense that a vocabulary list of terms and phrases based on these benchmarks would be a perfect fit for vocabulary instruction. Students who understand these terms and phrases should have a solid foundation for learning the more detailed information and skills needed to understand that content area.

In such content areas as science and social studies, much of the vocabulary students are expected to learn are words critical for acquiring new concepts or refining existing ones. Sometimes the new concept is described by a word new to most students (such as *photosynthesis*). In other instances, new words give more precise meaning to the concepts students already have, as when they learn to describe a geometric shape in terms of its *angles* rather than *corners*. And sometimes the very definition of a new word contains words that might be unfamiliar to the students, so all of them should be added to the vocabulary list. For example, only students who are familiar with the word *heredity* and understand what *hereditary traits* are will understand *genotype* and *phenotype*.

Students need to acquire vocabulary in a conscious and structured way so that they build the foundational understandings that are critical to the content being taught in the subject area. In a standards document, the benchmarks provide this structure since they create a scope and sequence of how the content will be taught. This structure is important: it is very difficult for children to learn more complex words without first learning the simple words that are the basis for understanding more complex material. The benchmarks provide this guidance.

This is especially true for young children. As they enter school and progress through the early grades, they are introduced to an incredible number of new vocabulary words related to the content they are learning. The words act as tools, helping students understand the key concepts that are new to them. The goal of teaching these words should be to help students understand them conceptually. This means that students will gradually gain a depth of knowledge about a word that allows them to use that new word in additional appropriate contexts because they are coming to understand the various dimensions of that word. This helps young children develop an understanding that moves beyond just labeling an object.

For example, consider the word *mammal.* A student may be able to label an animal as a mammal but not understand any of the characteristics that are attributed specifically to mammals and may not apply to other animals. Once the student begins to understand the characteristics of a mammal and then encounters the words for various specific mammals, such as *elephant, tiger,* and *bear,* she will not require the same level of instruction for each of these animals as was needed for the more abstract *mammals.*

Another reason for using the standards and benchmarks as the major resource for creating a customized vocabulary list is that it will help identify terms and phrases that may have a rather low frequency of use in everyday experience but are vital to understanding concepts found within the content benchmarks. For example, it is not often that anyone today encounters the term *trading settlement,* and therefore the frequency of use for that word might be low, but it is an essential vocabulary term for understanding the growth and development of the United States.

With the increased emphasis on aligning classroom practices with standards and benchmarks, publishers have made every effort to align their more recent textbooks to state standards. However, textbooks are typically written to align with standards from multiple states, and the degree to which the textbook aligns with a particular set of grade-level benchmarks may vary from state to state.

Although the vocabulary lists from the textbooks can be useful, they may not directly align with the benchmarks that you are responsible for teaching; therefore, the standards and benchmarks should be used as the primary source for identifying the vocabulary for your customized list. This does not mean that you should not use the list from the textbook but rather that the vocabulary identified from your standards and benchmarks documents should carry much more weight and be the primary point of reference. No longer should the textbook be driving what is taught; it should be used as a tool to help students learn the benchmarks.

Basic Words

Before reading the rationale for this source, it would be helpful for you to turn to the Appendix in this book and review the list of K–6 basic words provided there.

Although many lists identify high-frequency words, the list in the Appendix is somewhat different. It identifies words that are basic to the English language, that is, words in English from which other words are derived. The underlying assumption is that students who learn these basic words will be able to figure out the meaning of many related words in both oral and written language experiences. For example, *home* is a basic word for first graders. If they understand the meaning of *home* in the first grade, they will most likely be able to understand the words *homeroom, homework, home town, home baked, homemade, home grown, home schooling, nursing home,* and *homeward.* Understanding the word *home,* and with help from context, students will also have insight into the meaning of the words *homesick* and *home rule.* That's more than a dozen words they learn from learning one basic word!

How was this list of K–6 basic words in the Appendix developed? For many years, several bodies of research have identified words basic to the English language that could significantly affect student vocabulary development. The thinking was that by teaching students a list of basic words, the students would be more likely to understand new words that were related to those basic words in structure or meaning. However, most of the lists contained so many words that they could not reasonably be expected to be taught by a regular classroom teacher in one school year. In 1991, the Mid-Continent Regional Educational Laboratory (McREL) researchers studied that research and their accompanying word lists. They did a technical analysis of the word lists as well as numerous K–6 textbooks in all subject areas and four major standardized tests. From these resources, they identified the basic words from which other words can be understood, thereby condensing an initial list of 30,371 words to 6,768. The result is a basic list of the most important words and content concepts that students in grades K–6 need to know (Marzano, Kendall, and Paynter, 1991).

Since these words are "basic" words, many students may already know their meanings. Our concern is for those students who do not. These words might not emerge from a standards-based vocabulary list, so we have included this list as a resource for teachers to draw from.

Fiction and Nonfiction Students Will Encounter

In many classrooms, teachers independently select words for vocabulary instruction from the fiction and nonfiction that students will encounter in their language arts experiences. Some of these new words will be ones that students will rarely encounter, and others might be words helpful to students as they encounter new content in the classroom and outside school. Since there is a limited amount of time that can be allocated to vocabulary instruction, it is more productive to select words from the language arts experiences that would be most useful to the content that students are encountering now, content they will be covering in the future, and the kinds of words that will help them expand their vocabulary.

Most basal reading series produce a list of vocabulary words that students will be encountering, and the same thinking applies here as with books selected by the teacher. Not all of the words on the basal lists are of equal importance, and the same criteria can be applied to determine which of the words on the lists will be most useful to students overall. Again, if you had to teach all of these words, there would not be much time to teach all of the other content that you are responsible for teaching. Therefore, you need to be selective about which words you place on your customized list.

Certainly there are other books that students will choose to read both in and out of class, often referred to as wide reading experiences. Because students' selection of the books for wide reading is so varied, it would be impossible to identify those words and place them on your customized list. (We addressed this aspect of vocabulary growth in Chapter Five as part of incidental vocabulary learning.)

Words Related to Assessments

The emphasis on collecting data that reflect students' level of proficiency relative to the standards and benchmarks has been on the increase. In addition to state assessments, you may have other national or district assessments that students must complete. There is often vocabulary that is critical when taking these tests. It may be vocabulary that students must know to follow the directions in the administering of the assessment or vocabulary terms and phrases that are used within the test itself. If this is the case, be sure to include this vocabulary on your customized list.

In many cases, lists of words may already be available through the manufacturers of the assessment, so check to see where you could find these lists. If they are not available, you may have to rely on your own resources to compile this list.

A PROCESS FOR CREATING A CUSTOMIZED VOCABULARY LIST

We recommend a four-part process for creating a customized vocabulary list for your students:

> Part A: Identify the essential vocabulary that students need to learn to become proficient in the benchmarks for your grade level. These words form the standards-based vocabulary list.

> Part B: Identify the basic words from the book appendix for your grade level, and add them to your standards-based list.

> Part C: Identify the essential vocabulary from the language arts books and literature that students will be encountering, and add those words to the list.

> Part D: Add words related to district, state, and national assessments.

Each part of this process comprises several steps. In all, the four parts consist of six steps that you will need to complete. In addition to working independently, you can do this work with a colleague or gather together the teachers at your grade level for some short vocabulary-hunting sessions.

Before you begin, think about a format that you might use to collect the words for the customized list. Figure 6.1 shows a format one teacher used. Whether you use this format or another, it will be most helpful if you determine up front how to record the words for your customized list.

Once you have determined how you will record words, it is time to begin finding those words. To assist you, we have broken the process into parts and spelled out what needs to be done within each part. In addition, we have provided some practical tips on how to think through each step of the process. The sidebars by each part show an example of how one teacher worked through the process.

Part A: Identifying Your Standards-Based Vocabulary

Of the four parts of the process, Part A, which consists of three steps, is the most complex. Before you begin, you may wish to review the standards and benchmarks for the subject areas at your grade level. Check to see if your state or district has already chosen the key terms and phrases students need to know. If they have already selected a list of vocabulary words related to each of the benchmarks, you are in luck and can move on to Part B.

Figure 6.1.
Form for Recording Words for the Word List

Grade Level	Content Vocabulary	Basic Words	Language Arts Vocabulary	Assessment Vocabulary
5	Math			
5	Science			
5	Social Studies			

If no vocabulary lists have been chosen by your state or district, it is up to you to find those key terms and phrases that will help your students understand the content in the benchmark:

• *Step 1: Choose a content area.* Read the first benchmark, and think about the key vocabulary words and phrases that students need to know in order to become proficient in the benchmark. Perhaps some of the key terms are part of the benchmark. As you do this, you will go through a process of asking yourself what it is that is important in this benchmark. What *must* students know and understand? You do not ask yourself what it would be *nice* for them to know. You need to be intentional in noting what is important. As you do this, key ideas and necessary vocabulary become more evident.

• *Step 2: Move on to the next benchmark.* Repeat step 1 until you have identified and recorded the vocabulary terms and phrases for all of the benchmarks in this content area.

• *Step 3: Move on to the next subject area you teach.* Using step 1, identify the vocabulary for all of the benchmarks in each of the subject areas you are responsible for teaching. Add these words to your customized list. If you identify words you have already recorded on your customized list, do not add them again unless they are being used in a different context. For example, you may come across a word that has multiple meanings, such as the word *gas*. In science it may represent "neither a solid nor a liquid," but in social studies it may represent "the liquid that is used as fuel for vehicles." In this case, you may wish to add the word in both places and differentiate between the two meanings.

Part B: Add Basic Words to Standards-Based List

• *Step 4: Turn to the appendix, and find the list of basic words for your grade level.* Add any words from this list that do not already appear on your customized list.

You may be concerned that some students already know the meaning of some of these words. Chapter Seven deals with preassessing which words on your customized list students already know and which ones you will need to teach.

Ms. Marchbanks, a fourth-grade teacher, takes a look at the first physical science standard for fourth grade from her state standards: "Understands atmospheric processes and the water cycle." Then she looks at the first benchmark for more specific language and, she hopes, some vocabulary terms and phrases: "Knows that water exists in the air in different forms (e.g., in clouds and in fog in tiny droplets; in rain, snow, and hail) and changes from one form to another through various processes (e.g., freezing, condensation, precipitation, evaporation)." There, right in the benchmark, are some of the terms students clearly will need to know in order to understand the concept of the water cycle: *droplets, freezing, condensation, precipitation,* and *evaporation.*

Since this is Ms. Marchbanks's first year teaching the water cycle, she decides to ask her colleagues to help her think through what she wants her students to know and be able to do around the water cycle.

Ms. Marchbanks summarizes for herself the content knowledge she wants her fourth-grade students to have about the water cycle and how it affects us:

- Forms of water (*liquid, solid, gas,* or *vapor*)
- Processes *(evaporation, condensation, precipitation, freezing, melting)*
- What happens at each stage of the cycle
- Why it happens
- Examples in everyday life *(rainbow, dew, fog)*
- Uses of water *(drought, reservoir, conservation)*

Based on her knowledge of fourth graders, her conversations with her colleagues, and the science content, she chooses the following words as essential for understanding the water cycle and she adds them to her customized list. They form the first piece of her standards-based list, the culmination of the steps in Part A:

- *evaporation*
- *condensation*
- *precipitation*
- *freeze*
- *melt*
- *gas*
- *liquid*
- *solid*

At this point, Ms. Marchbanks decides to consult the benchmarks from the third and fifth grades. Knowing what has already been covered and what will be covered can help her narrow down her list. She sees that the words *freeze, liquid,* and *solid* would be taught in third grade, so she deletes those words from her list.

Ms. Marchbanks goes on to finish this process for all the benchmarks in all the subject areas she teaches.

Next, Ms. Marchbanks checks the appendix of this book for the fourth-grade words on the basic words list to see if there are any words that do not already appear on her customized list. She notices that the word *solid* already appears on her list, but sees that she needs to add three words from the basic word list:

- *dew*

- *absorb*

- *condense*

Ms. Marchbanks continues to add words from the basic word list that are not already on her current customized word list.

Part C: Vocabulary from Language Arts Experiences

Before you begin the steps for Part C, gather the fiction and nonfiction books that you plan to use in your students' language arts experiences. This might include literature, poetry, and nonfiction that you have selected or a basal reading book that you will be using in your classroom (or both). If you are using a basal reader, a list of the vocabulary terms and phrases that students will need to know is already available for your use.

- *Step 5: For each book that students will be reading, identify the vocabulary words that are critical to students' comprehension.* This does not mean you need to identify all of the words you think students might not know. The only words you would add to your customized list are those you think will cause confusion, will allow students to make multiple connections to words they already know (such as *gas*), and will expand students' understanding of a category of words. For example, you would add *tram* to a third-grade list since students already understand the category of transportation and some words in that category, such as *truck, car, bus,* and *automobile.* The addition of the word *tram* will increase their understanding of this category of words.

Now Ms. Marchbanks gets out her literature books and begins to look for the words that it will be important for students to know. She uses the following criteria to make decisions as to which of the unknown words that students will encounter in their reading will be the most beneficial for them to learn:

- Words for which students might not have any prior knowledge that are crucial to the story line. That is, the unknown word is central to students' understanding of what is going on in the story.

- Words that provide additional distinctions for concepts that students are already familiar with that could be used in other areas of the curriculum.

- Words that have complex or multiple meanings that students would have difficulty understanding. This lack of understanding would lead to their being confused regarding what is happening in the story.

Add the words you have identified to your customized vocabulary list. If there are any duplicates of words that are already on your list, do not add them.

Part D: Vocabulary from National, State, and District Assessments

• *Step 6: Select words related to assessments that you will be using.* Often school districts and states place sample test items on their Web site. If your district does not, you could contact the curriculum directors in your district and see what they have. In addition, you might brainstorm with your colleagues and use your collective experience to create a list. Determine if the assessment words you have chosen provide a list of the essential vocabulary students will need to know in order to take the test. Check to see if any of these words are already on your customized list. If they are not, add them to the list.

Since Ms. Marchbanks's district does not post any sample test questions or vocabulary words related to the standardized tests, she decides to ask her colleagues to brainstorm with her. They create the following list:

- *trace*
- *analyze*
- *describe*
- *summarize*
- *compare*
- *contrast*
- *predict*

Since none of these words appear in her basic word list from the appendix, literature books, or standards-based list, Ms. Marchbanks adds them to her customized list.

SUMMARY

At the end of this four-part process, you will have a customized list derived from the four resources we have identified. Keep in mind that as you and your students encounter new experiences throughout the year, you will find additional vocabulary terms that students will need to know. As you use textbooks in the various content areas, you may find additional words there. It would be helpful to keep a list of these words. At the end of the year, you could review the list and see if you wish to add to or delete from your customized list.

At this point, you probably have an extremely long list of vocabulary terms and phrases and may be feeling somewhat overwhelmed. Chances are you are convinced that you could never teach your students all of these words. You are probably right . . . but don't panic! In the next chapter, we address this issue and provide guidance on how to set up your classroom to make sure that students interact with all of these words to a greater or lesser degree throughout the year.

Deciding When and How to Introduce New Words

As Mr. Sperry finished his customized first-grade vocabulary list, he began to categorize the words that would require direct instruction versus those that could be taught through planned incidental learning experiences. When he realized that many of his words fell into the category of planned incidental learning, he really wasn't surprised. He knew that preparing students for reading was an essential part of the first-grade curriculum and there would be a heavier emphasis on words needed for general literacy development than on complex content-area vocabulary. He decided that it would be more meaningful to cover the words he had tagged for direct instruction during the appropriate units and lessons they aligned with because they provided a strong, natural context. But the long list of words for planned incidental learning worried him.

In past years, Mr. Sperry had provided a word wall for students to use as they engaged in various writing projects. He and his students had added words to it as the year progressed. Although the words were fairly simple, he felt that the word wall had been useful to students, especially in helping them learn how to spell. As he was contemplating the use of a word wall for this school year, he decided that he would use it to help students learn vocabulary as well as spelling. Rather than create an alphabetical word wall, he placed the words in semantic groups that related to the classroom experiences the students would be having. He created categories that described those groups and placed the appropriate words in columns (Figure 7.1).

Figure 7.1.
Semantic Clusters for a Word Wall

What People Do	Animals	Sizes and Amounts	Feelings	Food	Time	Things We Use
coach doctor judge lawyer nap	alligator caterpillar tadpole ant butterfly monkey mouse lamb elephant duck	gallon foot giant half heavy large measure mile	brave enjoy fear upset afraid happy	beef cereal cheese dough flour grocery sandwich vegetables cake	minute month noon always once morning next	hammer ladder oven scissors

Travel	People	Talking	Places	Water	Noises	Your Body
bicycle canoe helicoper	aunt brother parent sister uncle	listen speak whisper	country East North South West state	pour liquid	alarm sound loud	self head dress

Mr. Sperry decided that he would begin the year with these clusters and words and add to them throughout the year. In this way, he could incorporate the direct instruction and random incidental words that students were also learning by adding to the clusters that he already had in his classroom or by adding clusters.

As he looked at the rest of the vocabulary from his planned incidental learning list, he decided that he would divide these words into the four quarters of the school year and make sure students encountered each of these words at least six times throughout each quarter.

Mr. Sperry is creating a well-thought-out plan to ensure that his students are able to learn the essential vocabulary for the first grade. That is really what it takes. If you have created a customized list for your grade level, you need to develop a plan that allows students the opportunity to learn the words on your list. In this chapter, we will provide you support in these ways:

- Applying criteria to categorize the words from your list as those that require direct instruction or required planned incidental learning experiences

- Creating a plan that ensures that students have the opportunity to learn these words

SELECTING WORDS FOR DIRECT INSTRUCTION

If you have a vocabulary list for your grade level, you may be wondering how to decide which words are appropriate for direct instruction and which are appropriate for planned incidental learning experiences. To help you make this decision, we suggest that you apply a set of criteria that will help you determine which words are more complex or nuanced and therefore require direct instruction. The rest of the words would then be tagged for planned incidental learning experiences.

Not all words require the same amount of attention. Some are more difficult and require a deeper level of understanding than others. These are the words that require direction and structure to ensure that students gain understanding. To help you determine what words from the list will direct instruction, we suggest you apply the following criteria:

- Words that have multiple meanings or are found in potentially misleading contexts that would confuse students.

- Words for which students have no other words or no prior knowledge to determine meaning even within a context. This situation arises most often with content-area words, such as *photosynthesis.*

- Words that are difficult for students to grasp the meaning of and are frequently misunderstood.

Here is an example. Suppose that the following words were on your fifth-grade list: *matter, flotation, invade, photosynthesis, parallelogram, pardon,* and *perennial*. Which of these do you think students would need direct instruction on given the criteria listed above? We chose *matter, photosynthesis, parallelogram,* and *perennial* for the following reasons:

Matter: Students might know the expression, *"What's the matter?"* but have little understanding of how the world is made up of different types of *matter*. This is a word with multiple meanings.

Photosynthesis: The concept of photosynthesis is hard to understand, especially if it is explained by words like *chlorophyll, oxygen,* and *respiration*. This is a word for which students have no other words or prior knowledge that would help them determine meaning, even in a context.

Parallelogram: Children would be confused by the word *parallelogram* because in some cases it applies to objects that they already know by another name such as squares, rectangles, and diamonds, which in a mathematical sense, are all parallelograms. Switching from everyday use to technical use makes this word difficult.

Perennial: Although children can understand the idea that a *perennial* plant is one that lasts more than two years, they often get this confused with the term *annual*, a plant that lasts one year. This is a word that is frequently misunderstood.

Students could learn the other words—*pardon, flotation,* and *invade*—through the context of everyday experiences in the classroom. This is where you can rely on your new knowledge of planned incidental learning experiences: use a word multiple times over the course of a week; write certain words on labels and place them around the room for students to see in a meaningful context; or create bulletin boards that contain clusters related to the new words.

As you choose words for direct instruction based on the criteria we set out (see Figure 7.2), keep in mind that an essential aspect of direct instruction is modeling the strategies presented in Chapter Four.

CREATING A PLAN

It is most helpful at this point if you try to design a plan to make sure that the words from your customized list will be covered. Before you do this, however, you

Figure 7.2.
**Categorizing Words for Direct Instruction
or Planned Incidental Learning**

Vocabulary List	Direct Instruction	Planned Incidental
access		✓
adapt	✓	
adequate		✓
administer	✓	
allegiance	✓	
amble		✓
auxiliary	✓	
beacon	✓	
bleak		✓
bog	✓	
briar	✓	
brute		✓
bustle	✓	
civil	✓	

need to consider that your students might already know some of the words. This may be especially true of the words from the basic word list in the Appendix. If most of your students are already familiar with some of these words and their meanings, you will not have to schedule learning experiences for these words. If you find that there are a handful of students who do not know certain words, plan experiences specifically for them. Remember that there will most likely be quite a vocabulary gap among students; some will need additional learning experiences, especially those who have not been exposed to these words, such as ELL students.

Checking for Prior Knowledge

By now, your vocabulary list probably seems a little less daunting. We are aware that each group of students is unique and that their knowledge and skills vary from one year to another even within the same grade level. As you continue to plan for direct and incidental experiences, it would be helpful for you, at the beginning of the year or each quarter, to preassess students regarding the list that you have created. This can be a simple, straightforward assessment that does not take much time. It will help you diagnose which words on your list students already know. For example, the vocabulary assessment in Figure 7.3 could be used to find out if students had any prior knowledge of the words on their customized list. This quick assessment could give teachers valuable information that would help them make decisions about which students needed what kind of instruction on which words.

Scheduling Direct Instruction Experiences

As you consider scheduling direct instruction experiences for your students, you might consider the experience of Hannah Evyindsson, a fifth-grade teacher from Minnesota who is trying to determine when she will provide students with direct instruction on the words from her vocabulary list that require direct instruction:

Ms. Evyindsson begins by considering setting aside a period of time each day when students will learn a certain number of words. Ultimately she decides that they might get tired of having a separate vocabulary time each day. Besides, she wants to tie the words to the content that she will be teaching. She knows that direct instruction of words critical to new content is important, so she wants to tap into the everyday experiences that students will be having in the subject areas. Then she can help them link the vocabulary they are learning to the new content they will be covering. She thinks that if students can make this link, they will be more motivated to learn the new words.

After contemplating her choices, Ms. Evyindsson realizes that some of the words are not directly related to the content she will be teaching but

Figure 7.3.
Third-Grade Fall Vocabulary Assessment

Directions: Listen to the teacher read the word to you. Then decide what color you will use to fill in the first box beside the word.

Color the box   **red** if you have never heard this word
                  blue if you have heard the word but are not sure of its meaning
                  yellow if you know what the word means

Word	Color	Show That You Know It
anger		
article		
basketball		
bonnet		
bulb		
canyon		
chalk		
chunk		
clue		
command		
court		

If you have colored a box yellow, then in the box beside it, show that you know what the word means by drawing a symbol or picture, writing a definition in your own words, or writing words that have similar meanings.

require direct instruction. She therefore decides to teach the content-area words during the time she has allocated for the subject area they apply to and then set aside one twenty-minute period each week for vocabulary class. During this time, students will learn the words from her customized list that are not directly related to the content in the subject areas but require direct instruction.

Once she has made this decision, Ms. Evyindsson maps out on a calendar the lessons and units that she will be teaching in each quarter of the year and identifies which words from her customized list relate to these lessons and units. She then takes the remaining words that require direct instruction and determines which ones will be taught in the vocabulary class each quarter. As she reviews her plan, she realizes that the list is much less overwhelming than she thought. Now she needs to concentrate on what processes and strategies she will present to students to help them learn these words.

Ms. Evyindsson understands that discussing new words and exploring their meanings takes time, whether this is done through direct instruction or planned incidental learning experiences. She also sees that spreading out direct vocabulary instruction throughout the day makes the task of learning new words less overwhelming. She knows that making time for vocabulary sends a clear message to her students: learning new words and using them is important.

How many words students should be learning each day through direct instruction will undoubtedly vary from day to day depending on the new content that you present. But it is important not to spend so much time teaching new vocabulary that students do not have time to learn the content itself. The number of words that students learn through direct instruction will be determined by how much time you set aside for it each day. For example, if over the course of a day you typically spend fifteen minutes teaching vocabulary in math, fifteen minutes in social studies, fifteen minutes in language arts, and fifteen minutes in science, you could expect that students in each fifteen-minute segment could complete the steps of the process for no more than one or two words. Keep in mind that these fifteen-minute segments are probably integrated into the teaching of the content and are not separate, isolated sessions.

If you set aside this same amount of time every day, you could introduce as many as four to eight new words each day through direct instruction. In reality, you probably don't have time to do this, but at least you now have an estimate of how many words students could learn in such a time frame. At first, you may be concerned that students will not be learning enough new words each week.

However, remember that it is important to design a plan that organizes your vocabulary list in such a way that students learn words as they encounter them rather than isolated at the beginning of a unit. Also keep in mind that your students will be engaged in incidental learning experiences that will expand their vocabulary.

Scheduling Planned Incidental Learning Experiences

Obviously you cannot spend all your time teaching vocabulary. Research provides us with some insight into the number of new words that students learn each year, although these estimates vary greatly—from as few as a thousand words to as many as seventy-three hundred new words per year (Baumann and Kame'enui, 1991; Beck and McKeown, 1991; Graves, 1986). Learning even three new words each day is a big accomplishment for young children. A teacher might be able to achieve some of this through direct instruction but will need other avenues to meet these expectations. This is where the incidental learning experiences apply.

SUMMARY

In the previous chapters, we have discussed the importance of being intentional and systematic when it comes to vocabulary teaching and learning. We have also shared ideas on how to customize vocabulary lists and how to make distinctions between direct and incidental learning experiences. It is important to note that this information does not constitute a program, since we believe that teachers do best when they customize their teaching to meet the needs of their students. Rather, we consider our offerings to be the best, most effective, research-based practices.

At this point in your reading, you should have enough information to determine how and when your students will experience the words on your customized list. We recommend the following steps:

1. Reread the criteria for selecting words for direct instruction.

2. Go through the words on your customized list, and mark those that meet the criteria for direct instruction.

3. Create a calendar for the school year. Decide what units and lessons you will be teaching in each month or quarter, and identify when you will cover the words that are tagged for direct instruction. Write these words in the appropriate place on your calendar.

4. Look over the remaining words you have tagged for planned incidental learning experiences. Determine which of these words will be covered in which month or quarter, and add them to the appropriate place in your calendar.

5. Determine how you might preassess students each month or each quarter to determine if students already know the meaning of any of these words.

In Chapter Eight, we discuss the importance of gathering evidence of vocabulary learning from your students.

Assessing Students' Progress

Setting up a vocabulary-focused classroom can be challenging, as Ms. Breeze, a sixth-grade teacher, found out.

A few days before the beginning of school, Ms. Breeze had already spent considerable time choosing her word list. Soon her students would be back at school, and she was nervous about creating the best conditions for them to learn these words. She had already placed several semantic cluster maps strategically around the room that would act as a class record of the words tagged for incidental learning. Her plan was that as she engaged students in direct instruction around essential vocabulary, she would add these words to the cluster maps.

Ms. Breeze felt comfortable with the changes she was making to her vocabulary program, but she had several concerns. First, she wanted to help her students take more individual responsibility for keeping records of the words they were learning. She also wanted to begin collecting evidence that what she was doing was having a positive effect on her students' learning. She wasn't sure whether she should have formal vocabulary tests or just be keeping anecdotal records or both. She wanted to know if students were retaining what they learned over time and if they were becoming more proficient and independent in using the words and strategies she would be teaching as part of direct instruction. She felt that she had put a great deal of thought and effort into her vocabulary program, but wasn't quite sure how to track the results of her efforts.

ASSESSING VOCABULARY: NO EASY TASK

Documenting students' progress around vocabulary growth is complex, and it is not surprising that Ms. Breeze felt apprehensive. In the past, the traditional approach consisted of teachers' providing students with a list of vocabulary words at the beginning of the week, administering a test on Friday, and recording each student's score. Over time, these scores were used as a means to determine students' grades on their report cards. Additional evidence might come from external assessment, such as the *Iowa Test of Basic Skills, Comprehensive Test of Basic Skills,* or a state assessment, which typically had a section that dealt with vocabulary. Although the results of these external assessments provided some feedback to teachers, the feedback was often not as timely or as meaningful as it needed to be.

With the rise of the whole language movement, more emphasis was placed on the degree to which students were using new vocabulary in their writing; however, it was much more difficult for teachers to interpret this evidence and translate it into a grade. More recently, using rubrics for assessing students' progress has been popular, and there has been increased emphasis on moving from a summative approach of collecting end-of-unit or end-of-year evidence to an approach that also incorporates formative or ongoing evidence, including student self-assessment data.

Even with all these changes, assessing students' progress in vocabulary is not easy. As we have noted throughout this book, there is more to vocabulary learning than just adding new words. In this chapter, we focus on what we are really assessing when we assess vocabulary and how we can make vocabulary assessment informative for student learning and for our teaching.

WHAT IT MEANS TO ASSESS VOCABULARY

Children's progress in acquiring vocabulary is manifested not only in their ability to understand and appropriately use new words and phrases, but also in their expanding knowledge about words and the expanding repertoire of strategies they use when encountering unfamiliar words. It means that when you are assessing how well your students understand new words, you should also assess whether they are aware of and are using strategies that help them learn these new words.

Assessing Knowledge of New Words

When assessing students' knowledge of individual words, it is important to assess this knowledge across different contexts, that is, whether they can use the word in a different situation so that it has a different meaning. Relying on one specific context may lead to your overestimating students' mastery of the word. For example, you may try to assess your students' knowledge of new words through a comprehension paragraph in which a new word is surrounded by known words in a familiar context. In this case, students are often able to answer the comprehension questions correctly, even if they do not know the actual meaning of the new word, because they rely on context clues. Conversely, you might overestimate students' comprehension of new words if they can show appropriate use; for example, a student may write, "Pandas eat bamboo." But many students fail to provide an accurate definition because their meta-linguistic awareness is so low that they don't know what it means to define a word. So while the student used the word *bamboo* correctly, he or she cannot actually define it as a plant with a long, woody stem that grows in tropical areas. You may not realize that this student's skill in defining words is lacking because he or she can use the word in a context.

Assessing the Use of Strategies

Another part of determining vocabulary growth involves measuring students' ability to use the strategies that will make them more independent word learners. That is, you need to collect evidence regarding students' ability to apply and become more independent in using the strategies they have been learning through their direct instruction experiences. You can make vocabulary strategies the focus of assessment. For example, you could ask students to replace a word with a more appropriate synonym using a thesaurus or to infer the meaning of a new word by analyzing the meanings of its root, suffix, and prefix. You can also assess students' use of vocabulary strategies along with their knowledge of the words by first asking them what a word means and then asking them to explain how they came to know this.

MATCHING ASSESSMENT TO THE OBJECTIVES

Different words require different levels of understanding. For example, it probably would not take as much effort for your students to learn the words *cotton candy* as it would for them to learn the word *archeologist.* In other words, as you are trying to decide what assessment to use, consider how much understanding students need about any given word and how long it might take them to gain that level of understanding. This will help you determine what assessment would be appropriate. Obviously, the words you have previously tagged for direct instruction require more guidance and depth of learning than words you have tagged for planned incidental learning. Therefore, the assessments used for each of these categories should allow the student to demonstrate the required level of understanding.

When we assess students' progress in learning new words, it is also important to specify if we are looking at receptive vocabulary (words students understand when they hear them or see them in a text) or productive vocabulary (words students can use in conversations and in writing). We know that students have many more words in their vocabulary than they tend to use. We need to encourage them to use those words; then we need to assess how they are using them and find ways to give helpful feedback. To decide on the appropriate assessment, we need to identify if we are expecting students to understand new words as they hear them or read them or if we are expecting them to use these words appropriately in their own speech and writing. This distinction will help you identify an appropriate method for assessing these words.

In choosing assessments, consider whether you will assess vocabulary in isolation or as part of a larger reading, writing, or speaking task. For example, students may be able to explain the meaning of a new word yet not be able to use it appropriately in writing or speaking. They might not even be able to explain that same word if it appears in a text in which the context of the word is different from what they are used to. In addition, research indicates that we cannot accurately gauge students' productive vocabulary based on the size of their receptive vocabulary and vice versa (Read, 2000). It means that no single assessment instrument will measure all facets of vocabulary learning. It also means that you will need to collect evidence from multiple pieces of student work that demonstrate various aspects of how vocabulary is used within the context of the classroom.

CHOOSING ASSESSMENT APPROACHES

Students should be given opportunities to show what they know and understand through a variety of assessments. We are all familiar with the multiple-choice, true-false, matching, and fill-in-the-blank assessments for vocabulary. These work very well but should not be the only way students are assessed. Try assessing students' vocabulary development by collecting and evaluating data from vocabulary tests and performance assessments, collecting and analyzing anecdotal evidence from their writing, conversations with them, class discussions, and class presentations. Use individual student records of the words they are learning, observe their progress in engaging in the vocabulary learning process, and track their proficiency in using strategies presented during direct instruction. These approaches will be discussed below, along with examples of how to use them at different grade levels.

Regardless of which approach or combination of approaches you will be using, all assessment expectations and criteria should be clear to students. Students should also be given timely and specific feedback that is corrective in nature and helps them move forward with their learning. Assessment should be an ongoing and student-participatory practice. It should not be considered something a teacher "does" to a student but something students do to show that they understand the work they have been asked to do.

No single assessment and no single piece of evidence will be sufficient to determine if students are increasing their vocabulary knowledge. As you collect multiple pieces of data over time, you will begin to feel confident about the overall progress your students are making. We have created four categories to help you think about ways to assess students' vocabulary development:

- Teacher-created classroom assessments
- Anecdotal evidence
- Individual student records
- External sources

Teacher-Created Classroom Assessments

Classroom assessments that are created or scored (or both) by the teacher take various forms and can be used as evidence of students' progress. The common feature of all these assessments is that they are designed specifically to gauge students' progress in learning vocabulary.

Conventional Quizzes. Weekly tests can provide evidence about whether students are learning the vocabulary you are presenting using direct instruction. A vocabulary test that will be most useful is one that allows students the opportunity to demonstrate their understanding of words. Vocabulary tests that ask students to match the word with the dictionary meaning will not give you useful information. A more effective vocabulary test asks students to demonstrate their understanding in various ways. In the list that follows, whether students use all of these ways or just one depends on how the teacher sets it up (ideally, of course, students would get to decide):

- Writing their own definition of the word
- Creating and explaining a symbol that represents the word
- Generating examples and nonexamples of the word
- Drawing a picture that represents the meaning of the word
- Giving an example or experience that reflects the meaning of the word

You can get the information that you need in other ways too—for example:

- Give students a sentence that contains the word they are learning, and ask them to explain the meaning of the word within the context of the sentence.
- Ask students to describe how the new word is similar to or different from other related words.

Obviously, not all of these examples require students to write down their answer. The goal of the classroom vocabulary test is to help you find out if students have sufficient understanding of a word so they can use it in their speaking and writing and recognize it within written text. Because you want to know if students retain their vocabulary knowledge over time, it is helpful to test the children on important vocabulary several times over the course of the school year.

Performance Assessments.   There are three main types of performance assessments that will help you determine your students' progress in their vocabulary development: constructed responses, products, and actual performances, with the third category encompassing a variety of possibilities:

- *Constructed responses.* For older students, create questions as prompts so they can write sentences or short paragraphs in response. Younger students can respond verbally to questions you ask or sentences you read aloud. (For examples of these strategies, see the section in Chapter Four on direct instruction.)
- *Products.* Once students have multiple exposures to words, they can create diagrams and charts or complete concept maps and Frayer models (see Chapter Four). They can show what they know by completing these and adding information

to them as they learn more. Semantic feature analysis is an excellent way to have students note the words they are learning in a particular unit that are related to each other and to note the characteristics of those words in this matrix. When they have completed the matrix, they can discuss either orally or in writing what commonalities and distinctions they have discovered about the words.

• *Performances.* Performances could include dramatic or choral readings or perhaps a role-playing demonstration of the word or words. Students could videotape or tape-record their performance so that it can be viewed or listened to later. Other performances could include exhibits students put together or perhaps a poem or play they write that incorporates the words they are learning.

• *Using reading for performance assessment.* Have students read or talk into a tape recorder. Using the words for the week or the unit, they can say the word and explain what it means in their own words. They can also tell when and where the word can be used. They might wish to simply talk about something that interests them and incorporate the weekly words into their "rap."

• *Using group activities for performance assessment.* Pairs of students can play a version of Twenty Questions using a list of words of your choosing. The first student selects a word and writes it down. The second student should not see this word. The second student begins by asking questions to try to guess the word. The first student can only say yes or no in response to the questions. Younger students may have trouble coming up with twenty questions, so they can modify this with up to ten questions.

Students could also work together to write or tell a story using the vocabulary words. The words need to be used accurately, but do encourage creativity. While some group members recite the story, others could act out parts of it and even have pictures or diagrams to display at the appropriate times.

Younger students could work together to match pictures with words and give feedback to each other as they sort. They could match pictures of animals to their young or life cycles of plants, for example. Encourage them to describe the words as they sort and match and to use them correctly in context as they work on this activity.

• *Student discussions and conferences.* As you work with the whole class, small groups of students, and individuals in all areas of the curriculum, there are many informal ways to learn about students' vocabulary development. You just need to do a little planning and remember your goals.

Use your word list as a basis for discussions with students regarding their progress. These discussions will let you know what additional support students need and the degree to which they are becoming proficient in learning what you have been teaching them. They will also allow you to clear up any misconceptions students have about the words they have been learning. The discussions will help you see errors students might be making as they engage in the vocabulary-learning steps and strategies.

One way to facilitate this type of discussion is to give students a set of questions and have them share their answers with you. Exhibits 8.1 and 8.2 provide questions for you to ask younger and older students in conference situations or self-peer reflection. Students need to focus on their thinking as they learn and use new words. These questions may be modified to fit your needs and the needs of your students.

• *Teacher-student conferences.* Conferences can be quick and to the point by selecting a few words you want your students to know well. Have students sign up for a conference to talk with you about the words. Have them bring their list of words to the conference, and as they tell you what they understand about the word and how to use it, make notes next to the word to give them feedback on their understanding and use. You might also choose to use a scale of 0 to 4 that you could place next to the word, letting them know how well you think they understand and use the word.

Exhibit 8.1.
Assessment Questions for Younger Students

1. What do you like most about learning new words?

2. What is most difficult for you about learning new words?

3. What do you do to learn a new word?

4. How does this help you learn new words?

5. What could you change to help you be better at learning new words?

Exhibit 8.2.
Assessment Questions for Older Students

1. Do you think it is important to learn new words? Why?

2. How do you decide what new words you want to learn?

3. What kinds of words do you find most interesting? Why?

4. How is learning new words making a difference in how well you do in school? Why do you think this?

5. What strategies do you use most often? Why?

6. How do you know when you have mastered a word?

7. How proficient do you feel you are at engaging in the steps of the vocabulary learning process? What steps are most difficult for you? What steps are easiest?

• *Peer conferences.* Students can partner with their peers for conferences. For example, after a teacher conference, students who have correct understandings of certain words can partner with another student on those same words. The student who finished his conference with the teacher can act as the teacher and use the same procedure with fellow students. This is a wonderful way to reach more students than you could by yourself.

• *Self-assessment rubrics.* Another way to collect evidence about students' progress is to provide them with rubrics they can use to self-assess. For example, you could give students a rubric to help them determine their own level of proficiency when learning a new word (Marzano, Norford, Paynter, Pickering, and Gaddy, 2001). (See Exhibit 8.3.) Once they have scored their knowledge using the rubric, they can discuss their scores with you or other students. Based on their scores, they could also set learning goals to help them become more proficient at learning new words. Whether or not they are meeting the expected level of proficiency defined by the rubric, this information is extremely useful to them as learners and to you as their teacher.

You can also provide students with a rubric for assessing their own progress in using the various strategies that you present. Exhibit 8.4 provides an example of a generic rubric that you can adapt for whatever strategy your students are learning and practicing. Here again, we encourage you to have your students use self-reflection to think about their thinking as they engage in selecting and using appropriate strategies to remember and use vocabulary words.

Exhibit 8.3.
Self-Assessment Vocabulary Rubric

Vocabulary Rubic

4 The student has a complete and detailed understanding of the term. The student generates explanations and descriptions of the term and uses the term in context.

3 The student has a complete understanding of the term and generates explanations and descriptions of the term.

2 The student has an incomplete understanding of the topic or some misconceptions about the meaning of the term. However, the student has basic understanding of the term.

1 The student has so many misconceptions about the term that the student cannot be said to understand the term.

0 Not enough information to make a judgement.

Vocabulary Rubic for Younger Students

4 The student has a complete and detailed understanding of the term. The student creates explanations and descriptions of the term. The student can use the term in sentences.

3 The student has a complete understanding of the term and generates explanations and descriptions of the term.

2 The student does not completely understand the term. The student's explanation shows some mistakes about the meaning of the term.

1 The student does not understand the term. The student makes many mistakes when explaining the meaning of the term.

0 The student does not try to describe the term.

Exhibit 8.4.
Vocabulary Strategies Rubric

4 The student selects and implements vocabulary strategies correctly without any prompting from the teacher. The student can accurately explain the reason for using this strategy.

3 The student shows proficiency when selecting an appropriate strategy but occasionally needs some prompting from the teacher. The student has little difficulty correctly carrying out the strategy and can accurately explain the reason for using it.

2 The student has difficulty deciding what strategy would be most effective and looks to others to make that decision. The student makes errors when carrying out the strategy and has difficulty explaining the reason for using it.

1 The student rarely selects appropriate vocabulary strategies and makes so many errors that the use of the strategy is not effective.

0 There is not enough information to make a judgment.

Collecting and Analyzing Anecdotal Evidence

In addition to using assessments specifically designed to measure students' understanding of vocabulary words, you can gain valuable assessment information from observing students engaged in activities whose primary focus is not learning vocabulary. Anecdotal evidence may be the only way to see if students are meaningfully incorporating new vocabulary into their speaking, listening, reading, and writing. The downside of anecdotal evidence is that on the basis of a single anecdote, it is hard to come to a conclusion about a student's ability to use new vocabulary appropriately across different contexts. Therefore, this approach should be used in combination with other approaches. There are a variety of ways to collect this anecdotal evidence—for example:

• *Student conversations.* Engaging students in conversations with you or observing them with their classmates provides you with two excellent opportunities to assess their listening and speaking vocabulary. In addition to gaining an overall impression about the richness and variety of a particular student's vocabulary, you can use these observations to assess a student's understanding of a word or expression. For example, if a student asks questions about a word, uses the word inappropriately, or even appears confused at a joke where this word is a part of the punch line, you know the student needs additional help.

• *Student presentations.* As students make presentations, they demonstrate their mastery of the vocabulary related to the topic. You can use presentations to assess students' reading vocabulary as well as their speaking vocabulary since presentations are usually based on reading (both fiction and nonfiction) that students have done. As students read, they encounter new words they will need in order to prepare for the presentation. Observe whether and how they use the new words. After the presentation, ask the presenter questions and invite the class to ask questions. You can make the appropriate use of vocabulary one of the criteria on which the presentation is graded. You could also simply informally observe students' presentations with an eye for their vocabulary use.

• *Student writing.* Various written products, from journal entries to science labs and book reports, can be used to assess students' use of new vocabulary terms. As in the case of presentations, you may want to encourage students to use new vocabulary by making it one of your grading criteria. For example, Ms. Breeze, our sixth-grade teacher from the beginning of this chapter, could ask her students to write about a Greek or Roman god or goddess using three new vocabulary words to describe their character. As students' writing becomes more closely tied to subject areas such as science or social studies, appropriate use of content vocabulary becomes an integral and increasingly important part of their ability to demonstrate mastery of the content.

Students' Individual Records

Another way to assess students' vocabulary progress is through the use of the students' own records. You will need to help them get organized to do this, but the rewards can be powerful. We suggest that you use the vocabulary cluster walls from your classroom as well as the vocabulary notebooks that students have been keeping to assess progress in learning new words:

- *Vocabulary notebooks.*

Ms. Breeze was keeping a class record of the words her students were learning through the semantic cluster maps on her classroom walls. This helped her determine at a glance the new words her class was encountering throughout the year. However, it did not give her the evidence she needed to document the degree to which individual students were learning these new words, engaging in a vocabulary learning progress, or becoming proficient in the use of the vocabulary learning strategies she was presenting to them.

In order to gather some of this evidence, she decided to have her students create their own personal vocabulary notebooks where they could record the words that were the focus of direct instruction, as well as other words that were of interest to them. She thought this might be a good place for students to keep a record of their efforts to engage in the vocabulary learning process and their progress in using the strategies that were being taught. The notebook could also serve as a way to let parents know which vocabulary words students were learning and those they wanted to learn.

Ms. Breeze gave each student a three-ring binder and asked them to divide it into three sections:

Section 1: Words I Am Currently Learning

Section 2: Vocabulary Strategies I Am Learning

Section 3: Words I Am Interested in Learning

Since she knew that she would be teaching students the six steps in the vocabulary learning process, Ms. Breeze decided to create a graphic organizer (Figure 8.1) for those steps that students could keep in the front of the notebook.

At this point, Ms. Breeze began to give some thought as to how students would organize the first section: "Words I Am Currently Learning."

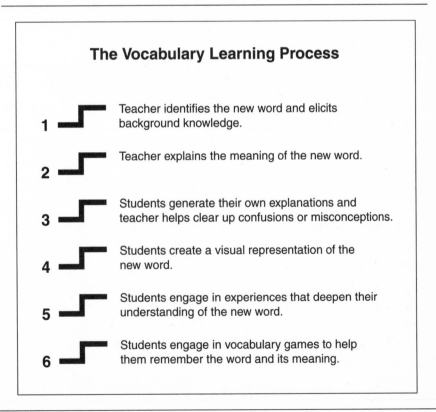

Figure 8.1.
The Six Steps in the Vocabulary Learning Process

The Vocabulary Learning Process

1. Teacher identifies the new word and elicits background knowledge.

2. Teacher explains the meaning of the new word.

3. Students generate their own explanations and teacher helps clear up confusions or misconceptions.

4. Students create a visual representation of the new word.

5. Students engage in experiences that deepen their understanding of the new word.

6. Students engage in vocabulary games to help them remember the word and its meaning.

She could have students keep their individual records based on the semantic cluster maps she had on the classroom walls or have them keep records within the various subject areas, like math, social studies, and science. She decided that for this semester, she would have them keep their records around the various subject areas since students went to a different teacher for art, music, and physical education. This way, students could have a place in their notebook for all subject areas, regardless of whether Ms. Breeze was teaching them. She also created a template that students could fill in for the words that they were putting in this section of their notebook (Figure 8.2).

Ms. Breeze knew that Section Two, "Vocabulary Strategies I Am Learning," would be the place where students would keep examples of the

Figure 8.2.
Vocabulary Template for "Words I Am Currently Learning"

My Teacher's Description	My Description
How I'll Remember This Word	Additional Experiences/Connections

SCIENCE

vocabulary learning strategies she taught and modeled. She created a different handout for each strategy and asked students to file them in Section Two. (For example, Figure 4.11a in Chapter Four shows the handout for the strategy of creating analogies.) This section would then become a resource for students when they were making decisions about which strategies to use to learn the words in Section One.

Ms. Breeze was feeling pretty good about the organization of the vocabulary notebook. As she thought about Section Three, "Words I Am Interested in Learning," she contemplated the planned incidental learning experiences that students would be engaged in. She knew that as part of wide reading, she would be asking students to gather words of interest to them. She also knew that if she was going to create a culture that valued learning new words, her students would need to have a place to note these words. In Section Three, she provided a place for students to record these words and then later, at an appropriate time, students could find out more about the words and add the information.

As we discussed in Chapter Four, students are more likely to remember the meaning of a word if they are asked to create a symbol or image of the word. Ms. Breeze wanted to incorporate that nonlinguistic representation into this third section. She finally decided to have students keep a running list of words they wanted to learn, and she would make available to them a template that they could use on their own to learn words on their list. Because she didn't want her students to get bored and lose their motivation for learning new words, she created a different template for these words (Figure 8.3).

• *Note cards.* Ms. Breeze had a clear picture of how she wanted students to create their vocabulary notebooks, but hers is certainly not the only way to do it. Another option is to have students use note cards instead of a three-ring binder. They can record the new words and their own definition or explanation on one side of the card and their nonlinguistic representation on the other side. They can then

Figure 8.3.
Template for "Keeping Track of Words I Am Learning"

Keeping Track of Words I Am Learning

Word	Characteristics	Examples	Nonexamples	Definition	Symbol

Word	Characteristics	Examples	Nonexamples	Definition	Symbol

use these cards as vocabulary flash cards. The note cards can be put on a ring or in a small box so that students will not lose them. This is probably a much easier system for young children than a three-ring binder. In any case, the notebooks or note cards provide a record of the words that students are learning.

• *Writing logs.* Students who are able to write can keep a log. Each time they use a word, they can write the date and state when and where they used it. This might be something that they do at the end of the day. You could structure this for students by selecting one or two focus words each day, and then students can learn from each other as they find and share new and different ways to use the word.

Make sure you collect these often enough to give feedback to the students. To avoid having to review too many logs at one time, have a few students leave them open on their desks at different times during the week so that you can quickly go along and read and comment on them. As you review students' logs, emphasize accurate spelling and the correct use of the words in different contexts.

• *Notebooks and journals.* Another way students show their understanding of words as well as strategies is by keeping notebooks and journals with symbols and images along with the written word. When students write a lab report for science or describe what they learned on a field trip or after reading a book, encourage them to use the notes they took along the way to generate information to add to this work. Students should keep this information in an organized manner in order to go back and add to their work and to use it to study. This process helps emphasize to students that words are not some list to be memorized in isolation but are important tools that will help them create understanding and increase learning.

• *Reading references.* Have students use sticky notes to mark places in their reading as well as their written work where they notice a word from their list. If students keep their vocabulary lists, notebooks, and note cards out as they read, they will have their own reference materials if they get stuck. As they read, students can refer to their own reference materials to get "unstuck." This improves comprehension as well as fluency.

Have students keep their important notes or pieces of work in a file for the entire year or semester depending on your class schedule. File boxes can be easily stored and accessed for both you and your students to add to. You may consider emptying a drawer of one of your filing cabinets or shelves if you have space and allowing students to store their work there.

External Sources of Assessment Information

While classroom assessments provide you with the most accurate information about students' progress in learning vocabulary, external assessments may be a valuable additional source. These external assessments are created and scored by someone other than the classroom teacher, and as a result they are not likely to match your vocabulary instruction as closely as your classroom assessments do. However, these assessments will show where your students stand in relation to other students of the same age and grade level.

Standardized Tests.   Standardized tests might include the vocabulary section from national and state assessments (such as the *Iowa Test of Basic Skills* and *New York Regents Exam*) or tests meant specifically for determining vocabulary growth, such as the *Peabody Picture Vocabulary Test*. Although information from these assessments can be useful, classroom assessments often provide more relevant and timely information.

Published Vocabulary Programs.   Designed to help students prepare for state or national tests, commercial vocabulary programs combine vocabulary exercises with assessments that can be administered and scored by the teacher. Typical assessments require students to match the words with their definitions, identify categories, apply the words' meaning in different situations, and answer comprehension questions. Since many of the words targeted by these programs are probably included in your customized word list (see Chapter Six), you should carefully consider the extent to which using these programs would be beneficial. We do not recommend that you use these programs in place of creating your own customized list.

SUMMARY

This final chapter has provided an overview of different approaches to assessing vocabulary:

- Teacher-created assessments that focus on vocabulary understanding and use in isolation (quizzes) and in context (performance assessments)
- Anecdotal evidence of vocabulary learning collected through observing students as they engage in a variety of listening, speaking, reading, and writing activities
- Monitoring of students' individual records such as vocabulary notebooks and writing logs
- Use of data obtained through administering external assessments such as standardized tests or commercially available vocabulary programs

You should view assessment not as something that takes time away from instruction, but rather as something that constantly informs instruction and makes it more effective. We hope you will be able to use the assessment information in this chapter as you begin to incorporate new vocabulary teaching strategies into your classroom. As you identify words for direct instruction or planned incidental learning, give the class a quiz on those words; before wrapping up a unit on magnetism, for example, make the use of the correct vocabulary words part of students' grades. These actions will keep you and your students mindful of the importance of a rich and robust vocabulary.

EPILOGUE

Vocabulary learning in the classroom should not be left to chance. Rather, it should be a thoughtful course of action that provides the underpinnings for academic success, not for just some students but for all students.

We believe that the teaching of vocabulary has been sadly neglected, and students with less-than-robust vocabularies have been at a disadvantage. We also believe that you have the opportunity and the responsibility to change this situation in your classroom.

Learning new words doesn't have to be drudgery and repetition. Rather, it can be enthralling, exhilarating, and even gleeful. Through your love of words and recognition of their importance in our complicated world, your students can be enchanted and even thunderstruck by the power of words. Through the structures and conditions you establish, they can increase their vocabularies, which in turn will increase their capacity to understand what they are reading, help them communicate more effectively, and enable them to better comprehend what people are saying to them.

Our hope is that this book has given you the knowledge and motivation to inspire and guide you in enhancing your current vocabulary program. At first, this might seem rather daunting, but when the learning is approached step-by-step, it can be accomplished. In *Bird by Bird: Some Instructions on Writing and Life* (1994), writer Anne Lamott tells the story behind the book's intriguing title. The words were her father's, spoken to her ten-year-old brother as he struggled to write a book report on birds. As each hour passed, the task grew more frustrating and more overwhelming until her brother was almost in tears. Seeing this, their father simply advised, "Bird by bird, buddy. Just take it bird by bird." Let's take that advice. Bird by bird or word by word, you can accomplish this one step at a time.

Appendix: A List of Essential Words by Grade Level

Robert J. Marzano, John S. Kendall, Diane E. Paynter

The identification of basic words has been of interest to educators for years, primarily because of the presumed utility of such a list. Given that basic words are considered to be those from which other words in the language are derived, a reasonable assumption has been that a knowledge of basic words within the English language will naturally lead to increased facility at learning the other words within the language. Specifically, it has been assumed that teaching students a small set of basic words could provide a key to understanding those words that are derived from the basic words (Becker, Dixon, and Anderson-Inman, 1980).

One of the earliest attempts to identify the basic words in English was Ogden's "basic English" (1932), an SSO [simple sign-on]-word lexicon from which all other English words could be derived. Unfortunately, Ogden's basic words were more like primitive concepts that cognitive scientists use to map the morphological

We thank Dan Jesse for his guidance and advice on the design of the study and the analysis of the data.

This publication is based on work sponsored wholly, or in part, by the Office of Educational Research and Improvement (OERI), Department of Education, under Contract Number 400–86–0002. The content of this publication does not necessarily reflect the views of OERI or any other agency of the U.S. government.

structure of nouns and verbs than they were like basic words from which the meaning of other words could be induced by the average language user (Schank and Rieger, 1974). A similar effort to identify the primitive semantic concepts in English was undertaken by Burger (1984), who focused on verb forms as the primary semantic structure within the English language.

Dupuy (1974) was the first to operationally define a basic word. Among other criteria, Dupuy listed the following: inclusion in each of four major dictionaries; not compound or hyphenated; not a proper name or an abbreviation; not foreign, archaic, informal, technical, derived, or variant. Based on a 1 percent sample of the four criterion dictionaries, he then estimated that there are 12,000 basic words in the English language. Following the Dupuy criteria, Becker, Dixon, and Anderson-Inman (1980) identified 8,109 basic words from a list of 25,782 words drawn from an updated version of the Thorndike and Lorge (1943) list. The intent of their study was to create a list of basic words that could be used as an instructional tool. Presumably a knowledge of the 8,109 words in the list would allow one to infer the meaning of the 25,782 (and perhaps more) words from which the list was derived. On the surface, such a list has great appeal. Reason would suggest that if coverage of these words was spread out over an extended interval of time (for examples, grades K through 12), instruction in the basic words would not be an overwhelming task.

Nagy and Anderson (1984), however, identified a number of fallacies in Dupuy's logic and, consequently, in Becker, Dixon, and Anderson-Inman's methods for selecting basic words. They noted that Becker, Dixon, and Anderson-Inman's use of rather strict morphological criteria for identification of basic words rendered their list invalid for all practical purposes, or at least invalid as an instructional tool. Specifically, Nagy and Anderson asserted that morphological relationships between words do not always ensure strong semantic relationships, at least from the perspective of the average language user. For example, following the Dupuy criteria, Becker, Dixon, and Anderson-Inman assigned the words *animism* and *animosity* to the same root word (basic word) *anima*. Nagy and Anderson noted that the average language user would probably be unaware of the word *anima*. Even if she were, they argued, she would probably not make a meaningful connection between *animism* and *animosity*.

In other words, Nagy and Anderson concluded that Becker, Dixon, and Anderson-Inman's 8,109 basic words are, for the most part, too unrelated semantically from the other words in the 25,782 corpus from which they were drawn to constitute an instructionally meaningful set. In fact, using a corpus of 86,741 words drawn from reading material encountered in grades 3 through 9 and referred to as "written school

English" (Carroll, Davies, and Richman, 1971), they estimated that there are 88,500 basic words. Based on this estimate, they asserted that any attempt to systematically teach and reinforce basic words would be futile since so many words remained to be taught.

Beck, McKeown, and Omanson (1987) offered an alternative to the Nagy and Anderson position. They conceded that there are many more basic words in the English language than could be reasonably taught in any instructional situation; however, they asserted that only a small proportion of the basic words would have to be taught to significantly affect student vocabulary development. Specifically, they noted that about half of the 88,500 Nagy and Anderson basic words would be encountered only once in an avid reader's lifetime, given the diversity of texts from which the corpus of study was drawn. In addition, of the remaining 44,250, only about 15,000 would be encountered once or more in 10 million running words. In short, Beck, McKeown, and Omanson concluded that although Nagy and Anderson are probably correct in their estimate of the number of basic words in printed school English, this estimate is not an accurate reflection of the number of basic words that students would be highly likely to encounter in reading. Their arguments suggest that a list of high-frequency basic words would be relatively short yet powerful in instructional yield. Since such a list could be very useful, this study attempted to identify a corpus of basic words that students would be highly likely to encounter in academic situations. In addition, this study sought to identify grade levels at which the basic words should be taught to students who do not already know them.

Although vocabulary words are commonly thought of in terms of grade levels, there is little agreement as to what a grade-level designation signifies and how to assign grade levels to words. Thorndike and Lorge (1943), for example, did not identify grade levels. Rather, they ranked words by frequency and then recommended that words between specific frequency ranges be introduced at specific grade levels. Harris and Jacobson (1972) identified the earliest grade level at which words appeared in at least three of six basal reading series used in their study. They assumed that the grade at which a word first appears in content reading material was the best indicator of when the word should be introduced to students.

Although there are variations on the theme, most attempts to assign grade levels have used the frequency of occurrence or first occurrence of words from a given corpus, usually drawn from a variety of types of text that students encounter. For example, Thorndike and Lorge's list of words (1943) was drawn primarily from student textbooks and magazines. Although almost all studies that we reviewed used frequency data from more than one type of reading material, no studies used frequency data for words on standardized tests. Consequently, this study sought to determine grade levels for the basic words identified using multiple frequency data that included standardized tests.

METHOD

For the purposes of the study, "words students frequently encounter in academic situations" were defined as words students will commonly encounter when reading content-area textbook material and in standardized tests.

Corpus

The initial word list used to generate the corpus of study was the *Basic Elementary Reading Vocabulary* (Harris and Jacobson, 1972). This list was derived from fourteen elementary textbook series (six basal series and two series each from the fields of English, social studies, math, and science) and contains 7,613 words. Because the list is somewhat dated, it was reviewed by sixty kindergarten through sixth-grade teachers, who added words they considered important for content-area instruction. For addition of a word to the corpus, the majority of the participating teachers had to agree. Words considered not relevant to current content were deleted. The addition and deletion process generated a list of 7,230 words. This list was then merged with words in Becker, Dixon, and Anderson-Inman's list (1980) of 8,109 basic words. Finally, the words found in the directions to the student and content of the following standardized tests were added to the combined list:

- The *California Achievement Tests* (CAT, 1986), Form E; Levels 10 through 20, inclusive
- The *Comprehensive Tests of Basic Skills* (CTBS, 1984), Form U; Levels A, B, C, D, E, F, G, H, J, K
- *Science Research Associates Survey of Basic Skills Objectives* (SRA, 1984), Form P; Levels 20, 21, 22, 23, 34, 35, 36, 37
- The *Stanford Achievement Test* (Gardner, Rudman, Karlsen and Merwin, 1981), Form E; Levels KI, K2, PI, P2, P3 I1, I2, A, T1, T2

In all, over 17,000 distinct nonduplicated words were found in the four standardized tests. The composite corpus generated from the aggregation of the sources described above contained 30,371 words.

Procedure for Identifying Basic Words

The corpus of 30,371 words was analyzed by two raters to determine which words were basic. A third rater was used to make decisions when the two raters did not agree whether a word was basic. Interrater reliability for the first two raters was above .99; that is, the two raters disagreed on fewer than one word per 100.

The criteria or rules used to identify basic words were the following:

1. Abbreviations were considered nonbasic (*etc., e.g.*).

2. Regular and irregular plurals were considered nonbasic (*houses, mice*).

3. Regular comparatives and superlatives were considered nonbasic, but irregular comparatives and superlatives were considered basic (*prettier* versus *best*).

4. Regular and irregular inflected forms (except for pronouns and some irregular verbs) were considered nonbasic (*walked, gone*).

5. Alternate spellings and pronunciations were considered nonbasic (*good-bye* versus *goodby*; *nothing* versus *nothin'*).

6. Proper names were considered nonbasic, except for months, days of the week, planets, the continents, the fifty states, and cities and countries that appeared with high frequency in K–6 reading material.

7. Formulas were considered nonbasic (H_2O).

8. Nonwords were considered nonbasic (*NATO*).

9. Foreign words were considered nonbasic (*señor*).

10. Ordinal numbers were considered nonbasic when they could be derived (from *fourth* onward); cardinal numbers were considered nonbasic when they formed a compound (*twenty-three*).

11. Feminine forms of nouns were considered nonbasic when masculine forms were available (*waiter* versus *waitress*).

12. Masculine and feminine forms of nouns were considered nonbasic, when non-sex-linked forms of nouns were available (*spokesperson* versus *spokesman/spokeswoman*).

13. Occupational titles were considered nonbasic when nouns existed describing corresponding fields of study (*biology* versus *biologist*).

There are some notable differences between the criteria listed above and those described by Nagy and Anderson (1984). First, it is important to note that Nagy and Anderson were interested in arriving at criteria that could be used to determine the number of distinct or basic words in printed school English. This study was aimed at producing a list of academically relevant basic words that would have immediate instructional utility using Beck, McKeown, and Omanson's (1987) reasoning. One necessary bias in developing such a list is that any word that cannot be easily derived from any other word by the average language user should be considered basic even though it is related to another word morphologically. Another is that categories or types of words that are frequently the focus of instruction should be considered basic. The rules used in this study reflect these biases. In the Nagy and Anderson study, all comparative and superlative forms were considered nonbasic. Since irregular comparative and superlative forms are very distinct from their positive forms (*good, better, best*), it was deemed necessary to include them in our basic word list (see rule 3). Similarly, in this study, inflected forms were considered to be basic except for pronouns and highly irregular verbs (see rule 4), whereas in the Nagy and Anderson study, no exceptions were made. Specifically, pronoun forms (such as *I, you,* and *me*) were considered basic in this study owing to their highly irregular nature. It was assumed that recognizing the word *I* would not necessarily lead to a recognition of the word *me* or other inflective forms. A similar situation exists for some verbs. Although there are many verbs that are irregular in the way that their principal parts are formed (*find, found, found*), only a few have such morphographically different forms that little relationship is apparent. In this study, such irregular verb forms were retained as basic words (for example, *bring, brought; go, went*). Similarly, conjugated forms of the verb *to be* were considered basic since that verb has such variant forms (for example, *am, is, are*). Proper names were considered nonbasic without exception in the Nagy and Anderson study, whereas in this study, exceptions were made for months, days of the week, planets, the continents, the fifty states, and cities and countries that appeared with high frequency in K–6 reading material (see rule 6). Cities and countries that appeared in *The American Heritage Word Frequency Book* (WFB; Carroll, Davies, and Richman, 1971) as frequently as any other word determined to be at the sixth-grade level within this study were selected for inclusion in the basic word list. In the Nagy and Anderson study, formulas were considered nonbasic, while in this study, an exception was made for numbers (see rule 10). Specifically, cardinal numbers were considered basic, whereas ordinals above *third* were considered de- rived forms or nonbasic. For example, *fourth* can be easily derived from *four, third* less so from *three,* and *second* and *first* cannot be derived at all from *two* and *one.* Again, cardinal numbers were considered such an integral aspect of classroom in- struction that it was determined they should be part of a list of instructionally meaningful basic words.

Any words not covered by the thirteen rules were then analyzed with regard to the extent that they were basic or nonbasic, where basic words were defined as those that could not be derived semantically or morphologically from another word.

Procedure for Determining Grade Levels

Once a corpus of basic words was identified, grade-level estimates were determined for each word. Specifically, all words in the corpus of basic words were found in the WFB, which contains 87,741 words taken from over 5 million words of run- ning text in material encountered by students in grades 3 through 9. The grade level at which each word first appears in the material used to create the WFB cor- pus was identified. Also, the modal grade for each word was calculated using the grade-level frequencies in the WFB.

These two data points provided a rough guide for estimating the grade level at which one might consider a word familiar to most students. The raters assumed that the modal grade levels calculated from the WFB represent those grade levels by which students should have a firm grasp of the word. Conversely, the grade level at which the word first appears in student reading material was considered to be the level at which the word might be understood by students with the aid of some direction or instruction. Using those two pieces of data as upper and lower limits, two raters initially assigned grade levels to the words. In their grade-level assign- ments, the raters sought to identify those levels by which students should be able to recognize and understand the words and be able to read and comprehend with- out the benefit of teacher aid the material in textbooks and standardized tests. Thus, the grade at which a word is introduced in reading material is probably too early, and the level at which a word most frequently appears is probably too late. The initial grade-level designations were then adjusted using the grade levels of first appearance on the four standardized tests used to create the corpus (the CAT, the CTBS, the SRA, and the Stanford) and the modal grade levels on these tests. That is, the two data points derived from standardized tests were used to validate the initial grade levels. Specifically, the raters determined the extent to which the initial grade-level assignments fit within the range identified from the four standardized tests. Any extreme discrepancies between initial grade-level assignments and the ranges on standardized tests were noted and grade-level assessments adjusted by the raters.

Five classroom teachers representing grades 1, 2, 3, 4, and 6 then reviewed all grade-level assignments. Teachers were asked to replace any grade-level assignment with which they did not agree with a grade level they considered more appropriate. Any word for which a new grade level was assigned by the participating teachers was then reviewed by the raters. If the two raters agreed, a change in grade level was made.

As a measure of grade-level validity, the final grade-level estimates were correlated with the first appearance and modal grade-level appearance on the WFB and the four standardized tests.

RESULTS

This appendix lists the 6,768 basic words derived from the corpus of 30,371 using the criteria described. The words are ordered by their final grade-level designations. Listed along with each word is the grade level at which the word first appears on one or more of the standardized tests used in the study. The correlations among the final grade-level estimates with the first and modal appearance of the words on the four standardized tests and the WFB for each word are reported in Table A.1.

Table A.1 indicates that the final grade-level designation (BASIC) was the most robust correlate in the matrix. Specifically, the range of correlations between BASIC and the other measures was .29 to .68. The low value of this range was higher than the low value of the range for any other correlate; similarly, the high value of this range was greater than the high value of the range for any other correlate. In keeping, the average correlation with BASIC (.47) was higher than the average correlation for any other variable in the matrix. The robust nature of BASIC is perhaps best illustrated when it is regressed on the other variables. The multiple R from that analysis was .83 ($N = 1448$, $p < .001$), and the coefficient of determination was .69. When multiple regression analyses were conducted using the ten other correlates in the matrix as dependent variables, the next highest multiple R using SRA (F) as the dependent variable was .77 ($N = 1448$, $p < .001$) with a coefficient of determination of .59.

Table A.1. Intercorrelation Between Grade-Level Designations

	2	3	4	5	6	7	8	9	10	11
1. BASIC	.38 (4,915)	.67 (3,401)	.68 (3,108)	.67 (2,806)	.62 (3,007)	.45 (4,861)	.33 (3,400)	.29 (3,109)	.33 (2,806)	.29 (3,007)
2. WFB (f)		.25 (2,889)	.26 (2,627)	.23 (2,384)	.25 (2,550)	.25 (4,861)	.12 (2,888)	.12 (2,628)	.13 (2,384)	.16 (2,550)
3. CAT (f)			.53 (2,398)	.52 (2,185)	.49 (2,331)	.34 (2,874)	.63 (3,400)	.17 (2,399)	.23 (2,185)	.18 (2,331)
4. CTBS(f)				.56 (2,094)	.50 (2,192)	.39 (2,614)	.19 (2,398)	.58 (3,108)	.22 (2,094)	.17 (2,192)
5. SRA (f)					.49 (2,037)	.41 (2,371)	.21 (2,185)	.19 (2,095)	.65 (2,806)	.17 (2,037)
6. STAN (f)						.34 (2,537)	.17 (2,331)	.14 (2,192)	.20 (2,037)	.67 (3,007)
7. WFB (m)							.26 (2,873)	.29 (2,615)	.29 (2,371)	.22 (2,537)
8. CAT (m)								.24 (2,399)	.25 (2,185)	.18 (2,231)
9. CTBS (m)									.21 (2,095)	.19 (2,192)
10. SRA (m)										.18 (2,037)
11. STAN (m)										

Note: All correlations in the matrix were significant: $p < .001$. BASIC = final grade level. WFB = *The American Heritage Word Frequency Book* (Carroll, Davies, and Richman, 1971). CAT = *California Achievement Tests* (1986). CTBS = *Comprehensive Tests of Basic Skills* (1984). SRA = *Science Research Associates Survey of Basic Skills Objectives* (1984). STAN = *Stanford Achievement Test* (Gardner, Rudman, Karlsen, and Merwin, 1981). I = first grade level of occurrence. m = modal grade level of occurrence. Parenthetical numbers refer to number of cases (words).

DISCUSSION

The findings in this study generally support Nagy and Anderson's assertion (1984) that there are far too many basic words in the English language to constitute a corpus that might be taught within the context of regular classroom instruction. Specifically, out of a 30,371-word corpus, 6,768, or 22 percent, were found to be basic. Although the probability of a word's being basic has an inverse relationship with the frequency of use of the word (Nagy and Anderson, 1984), one could induce from this study that there are many basic words in the English language, far too many to teach in any direct manner.

However, the purpose of the study was to identify a set of K–6 basic words that are commonly found in academic situations. Using the Beck, McKeown, and Omanson (1987) logic, providing students with direct instruction in a small set of words that can be used to determine the meaning of other words and are frequently encountered in materials they read, might have immediate benefits for literacy development. The 6,768 words in this Appendix represent such a list. Where 88,500 basic words would be impossible to teach, 6,768 in grades K–6 would not, especially if instruction were limited to students at risk in terms of their language development and limited to words they did not know. That is, instruction in the basic words could be limited to those students not performing up to expected levels in terms of their literacy development under the assumption that within the course of normal literacy development, the basic words would be learned incidentally or through direct instruction. Within this subset of students, instruction would focus on only those words students did not already know. Hence, for any one student, instruction would probably focus on a small subset of 6,768 basic words.

Of course, this study does not address such important issues as how instruction in the basic words should be accomplished. However, it does for the first time provide a corpus of basic words that by some measures appear to be academically sound and are also few enough to have instructional utility.

KINDERGARTEN

a	K	dog	K	look	K
all	1	down	K	mad	1
am	1	end	K	me	K
an	K	fall	1	mud	K
and	K	fan	K	my	1
are	K	fish	K	name	K
as	2	fly	K	no	K
at	K	food	K	not	K
away	K	for	K	of	K
back	K	from	K	on	K
ball	K	fun	K	or	1
bell	K	get	K	out	K
big	K	go	K	paint	K
bird	K	good	K	pet	K
blue	K	gray	K	pin	1
book	K	green	1	play	K
boot	K	groundhog	K	put	K
box	K	hat	1	rain	K
boy	K	he	K	red	K
brown	K	here	K	run	K
but	K	hill	K	sad	K
by	K	I	K	say	K
can	K	in	K	see	K
car	K	into	K	she	K
cat	K	is	K	sing	K
come	K	it	K	sit	1
cow	1	its	K	so	1
day	K	kitten	K	stay	K
do	K	little	K	stop	K

story	K	this	1	will	K
sun	K	to	K	with	K
take	1	too	K	work	K
that	K	up	K	yellow	K
the	K	we	K	yes	K
them	1	wet	K	you	K
then	K	what	K	zoo	K
there	K	where	K		
they	K	who	K		

FIRST GRADE

about	1	bread	1	could	K
add	1	breakfast	1	crayon	1
afraid	1	bring	2	cry	K
after	K	bunny	1	cup	1
again	K	bus	K	cut	K
ago	K	bush	1	dad	1
airplane	K	butterfly	2	dark	K
also	1	button	1	dish	K
always	K	cage	1	doll	K
animal	2	cake	1	dot	3
ant	1	calf	K	draw	K
apple	1	call	K	dream	1
ask	K	camp	K	dress	1
baby	K	cap	1	drink	2
bad	1	card	K	dry	1
bag	1	care	1	duck	K
balloon	1	cart	K	early	1
bark	1	catch	K	eat	K
barn	2	cave	1	edge	3
be	K	chain	K	egg	K
bean	1	chicken	K	eight	1
bear	1	child	K	elephant	1
because	K	city	1	else	K
bed	1	class	K	even	K
bee	1	clock	1	eye	1
before	K	close	1	fair	2
begin	1	cloth	K	far	1
behind	1	cloud	K	farm	K
best	K	clown	K	fast	K
better	K	coat	K	fat	K
bike	1	cold	K	father	K
black	2	color	2	feed	K
boat	K	cook	1	feet	1
both	K	cookie	K	find	1
bowl	K	corner	K	fire	K

firefighter	–	hen	1	lay	K
first	K	her	K	learn	1
fit	1	high	K	leave	1
five	K	him	K	left	1
follow	2	home	K	leg	1
forget	2	honey	1	let	K
four	1	hop	1	letter	K
fresh	1	horn	1	light	K
Friday	1	horse	K	like	K
friend	K	hot	K	lion	1
frog	1	hotdog	3	live	K
front	K	hour	2	long	K
fur	1	house	K	love	2
game	K	how	K	lunch	K
gentle	1	huge	K	mail	1
girl	K	hurry	1	make	1
give	K	ice	1	mama	4
glad	K	if	K	man	K
glass	K	inside	1	many	1
goat	K	jam	1	map	2
god	7	jet	1	may	1
gold	1	job	1	maybe	K
grass	1	joy	3	mean	1
guess	1	jump	K	meet	K
gun	3	just	K	might	K
ham	1	kind	1	milk	K
hand	K	king	K	miss	K
hang	1	kite	K	mom	1
happen	K	know	K	Monday	1
happy	K	lady	7	money	1
hard	K	lake	1	monkey	2
have	K	lamb	1	moon	K
head	K	land	K	more	K
hear	1	last	1	morning	K
hello	3	late	1	mother	K
help	K	laugh	1	mouse	K

much	1	people	K	seed	1
must	1	person	1	send	1
nap	2	pick	1	seven	1
near	K	picture	1	sheep	1
need	K	pig	1	ship	2
nest	1	place	K	shoe	1
new	K	plane	K	shop	1
next	K	plate	K	should	3
nice	K	pocket	K	shout	1
night	K	pony	1	show	1
nine	1	pool	K	side	K
none	K	pop	2	sign	1
nothing	2	print	K	silly	2
now	K	promise	1	six	1
off	2	proud	1	sky	K
old	K	pull	K	sled	1
once	1	push	1	sleep	K
one	K	rabbit	K	small	1
only	1	race	3	snake	K
onto	2	read	1	snow	1
open	K	ready	K	sock	K
other	K	ribbon	1	some	K
our	1	ride	1	song	1
over	K	right	1	soon	K
page	1	ring	1	sorry	1
pan	1	road	1	spell	2
papa	4	rocket	K	spin	K
paper	K	room	K	spot	2
part	1	rope	1	spring	K
party	1	row	3	squirrel	1
pass	3	Saturday	1	star	1
pay	K	saw	K	start	1
peanut	1	school	K	step	1
pen	1	sea	1	still	1
pencil	1	seal	K	store	K
penny	1	second	1	street	K

string	K	today	K	watch	K
summer	1	tomorrow	2	water	K
Sunday	1	toss	3	way	2
sure	1	town	1	Wednesday	1
surprise	K	toy	K	week	2
swim	1	train	1	well	K
table	K	trap	1	were	K
tail	1	tree	K	whale	K
talk	K	trick	K	when	K
tell	1	trip	2	which	2
ten	1	truck	1	white	K
than	K	Tuesday	1	why	1
thank	K	turn	1	wild	K
their	K	turtle	1	window	1
these	K	two	K	wing	K
thing	K	under	1	winter	1
think	K	until	1	wish	K
those	1	use	1	wolf	1
three	K	very	K	woman	1
Thursday	1	wagon	K	word	K
tie	1	wait	1	would	K
tiger	2	walk	1	write	1
time	K	want	K	year	1
tiny	K	was	K	yell	K

SECOND GRADE

able	2	believe	K	buy	K
above	2	belong	2	candle	K
across	2	below	3	candy	2
act	2	belt	3	canoe	2
address	3	beside	2	carrot	3
age	2	between	3	carry	2
ahead	2	bicycle	2	caterpillar	3
air	K	bit	2	cellar	2
alarm	3	bite	2	cent	2
alligator	4	blame	2	center	2
almost	2	blanket	K	cereal	2
along	1	bless	2	chair	K
angel	–	block	4	chance	1
another	2	blossom	2	chase	2
answer	2	blow	2	cheek	K
any	1	body	K	cheer	2
April	2	boil	3	cheese	K
August	3	bottle	2	cherry	2
aunt	K	bottom	2	chin	2
autumn	3	branch	2	chips	2
bake	1	brave	2	choice	K
ballet	7	break	3	choose	2
banana	3	bridge	2	chop	2
band	2	bright	K	chuckle	2
bandit	K	brook	K	circle	K
bank	2	brother	K	circus	1
bar	6	brush	2	climb	2
basement	2	bucket	2	coach	3
basket	K	bug	1	copy	3
beach	2	bump	2	corn	2
beef	7	bun	2	correct	2
beehive	3	burn	2	count	2
beep	5	butcher	3	country	1
behave	4	butter	3	cover	2

cowboy	5	during	2	flag	1
cracker	–	each	K	flake	–
crazy	3	eagle	2	flap	2
cross	1	ear	K	flat	2
crow	1	east	2	float	2
crust	4	easy	1	floor	K
cub	2	eighteen	7	flour	2
cupcake	1	eighty	5	flower	1
cupid	–	eleven	4	fold	2
dance	1	empty	2	foot	K
dear	2	enjoy	3	forest	K
December	2	enough	1	fork	3
decide	2	enter	2	forty	3
deep	2	evening	2	forward	3
deer	3	every	2	found	1
deliver	3	face	K	fourteen	3
design	2	fairy	3	fowl	K
desk	3	family	2	fox	1
dig	2	fancy	3	free	2
dinner	3	fear	2	fruit	K
direction	3	feather	2	full	K
dive	2	February	3	gallon	3
doctor	K	feel	1	garden	1
dollar	2	felt	1	gate	2
donkey	2	fence	2	gather	1
door	K	few	3	giant	3
dough	4	field	2	glasses	2
doughnut	–	fifteen	3	glue	3
dragon	2	fifty	3	gobble	3
drain	2	fight	K	good-bye	–
drip	–	fill	1	goose	3
drive	2	fine	2	granny	–
driveway	6	finger	2	gravy	–
drop	2	finish	2	great	K
dumb	5	fix	1	greet	3

grin	2	jacket	3	lock	K
grocery	3	January	2	lot	1
ground	1	jar	K	loud	2
group	2	jay	2	low	2
grow	K	jeans	2	luck	3
grumpy	3	jelly	3	magic	1
gum	4	join	1	magnet	3
hair	2	joke	2	March	2
half	2	jolly	3	mark	2
hall	3	judge	2	mask	2
hamburger	K	juice	3	meal	3
hammer	2	July	2	measure	2
handle	2	June	1	meat	3
hardly	1	keep	1	medicine	4
hate	3	key	2	melt	3
heat	1	kill	4	merry	3
heavy	2	kitchen	1	middle	2
helicopter	4	knife	3	mile	3
helium	4	ladder	2	mine	2
hide	K	ladybug	2	minus	1
hit	1	lamp	K	minute	3
hold	K	large	2	mirror	5
hole	K	lawyer	2	mix	2
hood	K	lazy	2	month	2
hope	2	leaf	2	most	2
hug	1	less	3	mountain	2
humor	5	lesson	2	mouth	2
hundred	2	library	2	move	K
hunt	3	lid	2	music	2
hurt	1	life	2	nail	2
hut	2	lift	2	needle	3
idea	2	likely	2	neighbor	3
important	2	limit	2	net	K
ink	4	line	1	never	1
island	2	listen	2	nineteen	5

ninety	3	peep	4	quart	2
noise	1	pepper	5	question	2
noon	1	perfect	2	quick	3
north	2	phone	K	quiet	K
nose	K	picnic	1	quit	2
note	2	pie	K	radio	3
November	4	piece	2	rag	2
number	3	pile	2	rainbow	3
nut	K	pink	2	raise	2
ocean	2	pipe	2	ranch	1
October	3	pizza	3	rare	5
odd	3	plain	3	real	2
often	2	plan	2	record	K
oil	2	plant	K	reindeer	3
orange	3	please	K	rest	2
outside	K	plus	6	return	1
oven	3	point	K	rich	2
owl	2	police	2	river	2
own	1	poor	1	roar	3
oxygen	3	popcorn	2	robin	4
pair	3	possible	4	rock	K
pancake	4	postcard	–	roll	2
pants	2	pot	1	roof	1
parade	K	pour	2	rooster	3
parent	3	power	2	rose	1
park	K	practice	2	round	2
parrot	2	present	1	rub	1
past	3	press	1	rug	3
paste	4	pretty	K	rush	1
pat	1	prize	2	safe	1
path	2	pudding	–	sail	2
paw	1	puddle	3	salad	2
peach	2	pup	4	salt	2
pear	3	purple	2	same	3
peel	–	quack	2	sand	1

sandwich	2	skate	2	strong	1
sauce	2	skirt	3	stupid	–
sausage	7	sleigh	7	subtract	1
save	1	slide	2	such	2
scare	2	slow	1	sudden	4
science	3	smart	2	sugar	3
scissors	4	smell	1	supper	3
score	2	smile	K	sweet	2
scratch	2	smoke	K	syrup	3
season	5	snack	6	tadpole	5
seat	K	soak	2	tall	K
seem	3	soft	1	tape	2
self	3	sound	2	taste	2
selfish	5	soup	2	tattle	–
sell	2	south	2	teach	3
September	1	speak	2	tear	4
set	1	speed	2	television	2
seventeen	6	spend	2	test	K
seventy	3	spider	3	thin	1
shake	1	spill	3	thirteen	3
shall	2	splash	K	thirty	3
shape	3	split	2	thought	K
sheet	2	spoon	3	throat	2
shell	2	sprinkle	2	through	1
shirt	2	stamp	K	throw	K
short	1	stand	1	thumb	2
shovel	2	stare	2	tick	2
shut	2	state	K	tip	5
signal	3	station	4	tire	1
since	3	stick	2	title	2
sink	2	stir	4	toad	2
sister	2	stove	K	toast	3
sixteen	2	strange	1	toe	2
sixty	3	strawberry	6	together	1
size	2	stream	K	tonight	2

tool	2	uncle	1	west	2
tooth	2	understand	3	while	K
top	K	upon	3	whisker	4
toward	3	upset	2	whisper	2
tower	5	valentine	–	wide	2
track	2	van	–	wind	1
tractor	3	vegetables	2	wise	2
travel	3	visit	2	without	2
treat	3	voice	2	wonder	2
trot	5	wake	2	wool	2
trouble	2	wall	1	world	2
true	2	wander	2	worm	5
trunk	2	warm	1	worry	2
try	2	wash	K	wrong	1
turkey	2	wave	1	yard	K
twelve	2	wear	2	yesterday	2
twenty	2	weed	2	yet	4
twig	2	weekend	2	yolk	–
ugly	2	welcome	5	young	2

THIRD GRADE

aboard	3	apology	7	bacon	3
accident	3	apostrophe	–	badge	3
ache	2	appear	3	balcony	5
adopt	–	approve	–	bald	7
adult	3	apron	–	Band-Aid	–
adventure	3	area	3	bang	7
adverb	3	argue	3	barbecue	–
advice	3	arithmetic	3	bare	3
Africa	3	Arizona	4	baseball	K
against	3	Arkansas	4	basketball	2
agree	4	arm	2	bath	3
aim	3	army	3	bathroom	9
airport	3	arrange	3	batter	4
Alabama	5	arrive	3	battery	4
Alaska	3	arrow	3	bead	3
album	5	art	3	beak	5
alert	4	article	5	beam	3
alley	6	Asia	4	beard	7
allow	5	Atlantic	3	beast	3
alphabet	4	attack	K	beat	1
already	K	attention	3	beauty	3
although	3	attic	5	beaver	3
ambulance	6	attitude	5	become	3
America	3	Australia	4	beetle	–
among	3	author	3	beg	–
amount	3	autograph	–	being	3
amuse	3	automobile	3	belly	3
anger	5	avenue	4	bench	3
announce	3	award	3	bend	2
annoy	5	aware	5	beneath	4
Antarctica	5	awful	3	berry	4
anxious	3	awhile	4	bet	3
apart	3	babe	5	Bethlehem	–
apartment	K	baboon	–	beware	3
ape	6	backward	6	bib	–

bible	–	bulb	5	ceiling	2
bill	K	bum	–	celebrate	2
birth	3	bunch	4	celery	6
bitter	5	bundle	3	cell	5
blackboard	–	bunk	–	cemetery	7
bleed	3	burglar	–	certain	3
blend	5	burro	3	chalk	5
blink	4	burst	4	chalkboard	7
bloom	3	bury	–	change	2
blot	2	business	3	charge	2
board	2	busy	3	chart	3
boast	3	buzz	–	cheat	7
bone	3	cab	3	check	2
bonnet	3	cabin	3	cheep	–
born	2	cactus	4	chest	3
borrow	5	California	4	chew	3
boss	3	calm	3	Chicago	3
bother	4	camera	3	chief	3
bounce	4	canyon	3	chili	–
bow	3	cape	6	chimney	3
bowling	6	capital	2	chimpanzee	4
bracelet	2	captain	3	chipmunk	–
braid	1	cardboard	3	chocolate	3
brain	5	caribou	3	chunk	–
breath	3	carol	1	church	3
breeze	2	carpenter	4	churn	3
brick	3	carpet	3	clam	3
broke	2	cartoon	5	clap	3
broom	K	carve	3	claw	3
brownie	3	case	2	clay	2
bubble	3	castle	2	clean	1
buckle	4	cattail	–	clear	2
bud	4	cattle	4	clever	3
buffalo	3	cause	2	cliff	2
buggy	–	caution	3	clip	3
build	2	caw	2	clop	–

clothing	3	county	3	Dallas	4
clover	5	courage	4	damp	4
club	4	course	4	dandelion	–
cluck	–	court	4	danger	2
clue	2	cowhand	–	dare	3
coast	4	cozy	3	dash	2
cob	2	crab	1	daughter	4
cocoon	–	crack	3	dead	4
code	7	craft	4	deal	3
coin	3	cranberry	–	deck	3
collar	4	crank	9	Delaware	3
Colorado	4	crash	3	delicious	3
colt	3	crawl	3	delight	6
column	4	cream	3	denominator	6
comb	3	creature	3	dent	5
comfort	4	creek	2	Denver	3
comma	–	creep	3	department	3
command	3	cricket	K	describe	4
common	4	crisp	7	desert	1
community	3	crocodile	4	desire	3
company	3	crooked	2	dessert	4
complain	3	crop	3	devil	11
complete	2	crowd	1	diamond	4
cone	1	crown	3	diaper	6
Connecticut	5	cruel	4	dictionary	3
consonant	–	cube	2	die	3
content	3	cucumber	–	difficult	4
contest	2	curious	3	digit	3
continue	3	curl	2	dim	4
cool	2	curtain	5	dime	4
copper	4	curve	3	dinosaur	4
coral	4	customer	3	direct	5
corral	4	cute	4	dirt	2
cost	3	daffodil	4	discover	4
costume	3	dairy	4	distant	3
cotton	3	daisy	3	disturb	3

dock	K	erase	6	firecracker	–
dodge	4	errand	–	firehouse	4
double	3	escape	2	fireworks	6
downtown	3	Europe	–	firm	2
dozen	3	ever	3	fist	3
drag	5	evil	4	flame	4
drawer	1	exact	3	flash	2
dread	6	exam	7	flee	5
drift	4	excite	9	flop	–
drown	–	exclaim	4	Florida	3
drowsy	9	excuse	4	flow	3
drug	3	exit	3	flush	7
drugstore	5	experiment	4	flutter	10
drum	1	explain	5	fog	3
dull	3	explore	3	foil	7
dump	4	extra	3	folder	3
dust	K	fact	3	fool	3
dwarf	7	factory	3	football	4
eager	4	faint	3	force	3
eardrum	–	fake	6	forever	2
earn	3	falcon	7	forgive	6
earth	3	false	2	form	2
either	4	familiar	4	forth	3
elastic	6	faucet	5	fossil	3
elbow	–	fault	3	fountain	3
electric	3	feast	3	foursquare	–
elementary	4	fellow	6	frame	9
elf	3	female	4	freeze	4
elm	5	fern	3	frost	4
encyclopedia	4	fib	–	frown	2
enemy	3	fiction	3	fry	–
energy	3	fierce	3	fudge	3
engine	3	fife	–	fuel	3
entertain	4	figure	3	fulcrum	11
entrance	6	final	5	garage	3
equator	3	fir	4	garbage	4

gas	3	hangar	–	hound	3
gasp	–	harbor	3	Houston	6
gaze	4	harm	3	howl	3
Georgia	2	harp	3	hum	–
germ	5	harvest	3	human	4
germinate	11	hatch	3	hunger	4
ghost	2	Hawaii	7	hurrah	–
gift	1	hawk	3	husband	3
giggle	–	hay	3	husky	6
giraffe	4	headline	–	hydrant	–
glide	4	heap	4	icicle	3
globe	4	heart	3	Idaho	6
glove	5	heel	2	identify	4
goodnight	4	height	3	ill	3
gorilla	5	hell	–	Illinois	5
gown	5	helmet	–	impossible	5
grab	5	hem	–	inch	3
grade	3	herd	3	indeed	3
graham	7	hero	4	index	5
grain	5	hibernate	6	Indiana	5
grand	3	highway	3	indoors	4
grandparent	–	hip	7	inn	3
grape	8	hippopotamus	5	insect	5
grapefruit	11	hire	3	instead	3
graph	3	hive	3	instrument	3
growl	–	hollow	3	interest	3
grown-up	–	holster	–	invite	3
guard	4	honest	4	Iowa	5
guest	4	honk	–	iron	3
guitar	3	honor	3	item	3
gull	2	hook	4	jail	5
gulp	–	hoop	–	jeep	7
habit	3	hopscotch	5	jerk	3
hamster	3	hose	2	jigsaw	–
handkerchief	4	hospital	3	jingle	5
handsome	4	hotel	3	joint	3

journey	3	lie	3	margarine	6
jungle	3	lighthouse	3	margin	9
kangaroo	4	lightning	6	market	3
Kansas	9	lilac	–	marry	6
kennel	–	limb	3	marshal	11
Kentucky	4	lip	4	marshmallow	6
kick	2	liquid	4	Maryland	5
kindergarten	–	list	3	Massachusetts	5
kingdom	3	liter	2	mat	8
kiss	–	lizard	3	match	K
kit	5	load	3	matter	4
knee	2	loaf	2	mayor	3
kneel	9	lobster	5	meadow	2
knock	2	log	2	medal	7
knot	2	lollipop	–	member	4
label	2	lone	2	mention	5
lace	3	loop	3	meow	3
lad	2	loose-leaf	9	message	2
lane	2	Los Angeles	–	metal	3
language	K	lose	1	meter	2
lap	4	Louisiana	4	method	4
larva	3	lullaby	–	Miami	1
lasso	–	lump	3	Michigan	5
law	3	machine	3	microscope	3
lawn	3	magazine	3	microwave	3
lead	2	maid	3	midget	–
leak	6	main	4	mild	4
lean	3	Maine	5	mill	3
least	3	major	3	million	3
leather	3	makeup	6	mind	4
lemon	3	male	5	Minnesota	5
length	3	mall	6	Mississippi	4
leopard	3	mammal	3	Missouri	5
lettuce	3	manhole	–	mist	7
level	3	Manila	–	mistake	2
lick	–	manner	6	moan	2

modern	4	New York	–	ought	3
modest	2	news	3	outdoors	3
mold	3	nickel	4	oval	9
moment	2	nickname	6	overhead	5
monster	3	niece	8	ox	9
Montana	4	nimble	–	Pacific	4
moo	–	nobody	3	pack	K
moose	4	nod	–	paddle	–
mosquito	5	noodle	5	pageant	6
moss	4	North America	–	pail	3
motel	–	North Carolina	–	pain	2
moth	4	North Dakota	–	pajamas	3
motor	4	notice	4	pal	9
mound	2	noun	4	palace	3
mow	–	numeral	3	pale	3
mulberry	–	nurse	2	palm	3
mule	4	o'clock	1	pane	6
mumps	–	oak	3	pant	3
museum	3	oatmeal	–	parka	4
mush	2	obey	4	partridge	–
mushroom	3	object	3	passage	3
mutter	4	offer	4	pasture	6
mystery	3	office	2	patch	K
narrow	2	officer	3	pattern	3
nation	4	Ohio	5	peacock	12
neat	2	okay	5	peas	3
Nebraska	5	Oklahoma	8	pedal	6
neck	2	olive	3	peek	–
necklace	2	onion	3	penguin	4
neither	5	opinion	3	Pennsylvania	3
nephew	3	opposite	3	perhaps	3
nervous	3	orbit	2	perimeter	3
Nevada	8	orchard	4	period	3
New Hampshire	–	order	3	pest	3
New Jersey	–	Oregon	2	petal	5
New Mexico	–	otter	4	piano	3

pigeon	3	produce	3	reason	2
pilgrim	9	professor	3	recess	5
pillow	2	pronoun	–	recite	2
pilot	4	pronounce	4	rectangle	4
pine	3	proper	2	refuse	3
pint	3	protect	2	regular	4
pioneer	4	protest	5	relax	3
pirate	5	prove	4	relief	2
pistil	5	provide	3	religion	4
pitch	3	puff	2	remain	1
pitcher	3	pump	3	remember	3
planet	3	pumpkin	4	remind	3
plastic	3	punish	3	remove	3
plenty	3	pupil	4	rent	7
plow	3	puppet	2	repair	1
plug	4	pure	4	reply	2
poem	5	purr	5	report	3
poke	4	purse	3	reptile	3
pole	2	pus	–	respect	4
polite	3	puzzle	11	restaurant	5
pollen	4	quarter	3	reward	3
pond	3	queen	6	rhinoceros	6
poplar	3	queer	–	Rhode Island	–
poppy	–	quicksand	–	rhyme	7
porch	3	quite	4	rhythm	9
post	4	quiz	8	rib	2
poster	5	radish	4	rice	3
potato	3	railroad	3	rid	6
pound	4	raisin	–	riddle	3
praise	2	rake	5	rink	2
pray	–	range	5	rip	3
prepare	2	raspberry	–	ripe	2
president	3	rat	4	ripple	4
pretend	3	rather	3	roam	2
prince	3	reach	2	roast	3
problem	3	rear	8	rob	2

robe	5	select	2	sill	–
robot	7	sense	2	silver	3
Rockies	–	sentence	2	simple	2
rod	6	separate	5	sin	–
rodeo	3	serious	3	single	4
root	3	serve	3	sip	12
rubber	3	settle	2	sir	4
rude	3	several	3	skeleton	3
ruin	4	sew	3	ski	11
rule	3	shade	2	skill	5
sack	5	shadow	5	skin	4
saddle	5	share	5	skip	9
sale	K	sharp	2	skunk	3
sample	K	shave	–	skyscraper	5
San Francisco	–	shed	5	slap	3
sap	3	shelf	2	slave	3
satin	–	shelter	4	sleeve	5
satisfy	5	shepherd	3	slice	5
saucer	–	sheriff	3	slime	3
scale	K	shine	2	slowpoke	–
scar	2	shiver	11	slumber	7
scarf	3	shock	7	smash	–
scatter	4	shoot	2	smooth	2
schedule	6	shore	3	snap	3
scold	3	shorts	7	sneeze	4
scoop	7	shove	4	sniff	3
scrapbook	–	shrimp	3	snob	–
scrape	4	shrink	3	soap	2
scream	4	shy	4	soar	2
screen	6	sick	3	sob	–
scribble	–	sidewalk	2	soda	4
scrub	–	sigh	K	soil	2
search	3	sight	4	soldier	4
secret	2	signature	7	son	3
section	3	silent	3	sort	5
seize	4	silk	4	sour	3

South Carolina	–	straight	3	teaspoon	4
South Dakota	–	strap	4	telephone	3
sow	7	straw	12	temperature	3
space	3	strike	3	tender	3
spank	–	strip	5	Tennessee	5
spare	3	stripe	4	tent	3
spark	–	student	3	terrible	2
special	1	study	3	terror	3
speech	3	stuff	5	tethe	–
spoil	3	substance	3	Texas	1
spray	6	suit	4	thermometer	3
spy	3	sundae	–	thick	2
square	3	supermarket	7	thief	3
squawk	–	surface	3	thirst	3
squeak	K	swallow	4	though	2
squeal	–	sweater	3	thousand	3
squeeze	3	sweep	2	thread	3
stable	5	swing	K	thunder	3
stack	2	swirl	3	ticket	K
stairs	2	swish	–	tickle	K
stamen	5	switch	3	tight	4
starfish	5	sword	3	tights	–
starve	7	symbol	3	till	2
statue	3	system	4	tin	4
steal	5	tablespoon	6	tinfoil	–
steam	3	taco	5	ting	–
steer	3	tag	4	toboggan	–
stem	4	tale	3	tomato	3
stew	4	tan	3	ton	3
sticker	4	tap	3	tongue	4
stiff	3	task	5	tortoise	–
stocking	–	taxi	–	touch	2
stomach	4	tea	2	touchdown	9
stone	1	team	3	towel	4
stool	3	teapot	4	trace	2
storm	2	tease	9	trade	5

traffic	3	velvet	9	whole	3
trail	2	verb	4	whoop	–
trailer	3	Vermont	5	whoosh	–
trash	4	vest	3	wicked	4
tray	3	village	4	wife	9
treasure	3	violin	3	wig	1
tremble	3	Virginia	5	wiggle	–
triangle	3	vowel	4	willow	3
tribe	2	voyage	3	win	3
trickle	–	waffle	–	windmill	9
troll	–	wag	3	wink	2
trust	3	wail	5	wipe	3
tub	K	waist	3	wire	1
tube	3	waiter	8	Wisconsin	5
tug	2	war	2	witch	4
tulip	4	warn	3	within	5
tune	6	Washington	2	wood	3
tunnel	3	waste	2	woodpecker	4
twin	1	watermelon	4	worse	3
twist	4	weak	3	worst	3
type	3	weary	2	worth	2
ukulele	–	weather	3	wound	9
umbrella	5	wed	–	wow	–
underneath	4	weep	2	wrap	3
unit	3	weigh	3	wreck	3
United States	–	West Virginia	–	wriggle	–
unless	3	wheat	3	wrist	3
upward	2	wheel	4	Wyoming	5
usual	3	wheelbarrow	–	yarn	3
Utah	7	whether	5	yawn	3
vacant	3	whimper	–	yeast	6
vacation	3	whip	–	zebra	9
valley	4	whir	–	zip	11
value	4	whistle	4	zoom	–

FOURTH GRADE

abbreviate	2	anniversary	5	awe	7
absent	4	annual	4	awkward	5
absorb	4	antelope	–	axe	–
accent	5	anthem	–	axle	4
accept	3	antonym	–	babble	–
accordion	–	appetite	4	background	4
accuse	4	applaud	5	balance	3
ace	3	appreciate	5	bale	–
acid	3	approach	2	ballad	7
acorn	–	approximate	3	ballpoint	5
acrobat	6	apricot	7	ballroom	–
actual	3	aquarium	3	Baltic	7
adjective	4	arch	4	bamboo	5
adjust	6	arctic	3	bandage	5
admire	3	ark	3	banjo	–
admit	6	arrest	–	banner	4
affair	7	artificial	4	banquet	3
afford	3	ash	7	bargain	4
agriculture	6	aspen	–	barrel	4
aid	3	aspirin	3	barrow	–
airline	4	assign	6	barter	–
aisle	5	assortment	8	base	3
alfalfa	7	athlete	4	basic	4
algae	5	Atlanta	3	basin	4
almanac	5	atlas	4	bat	1
aloud	5	atmosphere	5	batch	–
altitude	4	atom	4	baton	–
aluminum	4	attach	3	battle	4
amaze	4	attend	4	bawl	–
ambush	–	attract	4	bay	K
anchor	4	audience	4	beagle	5
Anchorage	–	auditorium	4	bedspread	–
ancient	3	auto	5	beer	–
Andes	4	average	3	beet	3
ankle	5	avoid	4	behold	–

beige	–	brake	–	canary	5
belch	–	brand	4	cancel	7
beyond	6	brass	5	cane	5
bibliography	6	breast	7	capable	4
bid	4	brew	6	capacity	4
billion	6	bride	5	capillary	–
biography	7	brief	3	capitol	7
birch	–	brilliant	4	capsule	4
blacksmith	4	brim	4	capture	3
blade	6	brisk	4	caramel	–
blank	2	broad	3	carbohydrate	7
blast	5	bronze	5	carbon	3
blaze	4	brow	4	career	5
bleacher	–	bruise	4	carnation	–
bleat	–	buddy	–	carnival	3
blind	4	budge	2	carriage	8
blizzard	5	budget	5	carton	3
blood	5	buffet	–	cartwheel	–
blouse	–	bull	7	cash	4
blurt	–	bulldog	5	casserole	6
blush	7	bullet	6	cassette	7
bobsled	–	bulletin	4	cast	K
bold	5	bully	7	catsup	–
bomb	–	buoy	–	cauliflower	10
bonus	6	burp	–	cavern	–
bookworm	4	burrow	5	cedar	7
booth	4	bushel	9	cello	–
border	4	butler	–	cellophane	–
Boston	3	butte	–	Celsius	5
bough	–	buttercup	–	cement	3
boulder	4	cabbage	6	Centigrade	–
bound	6	cable	4	centipede	–
bounty	4	caboose	–	century	4
bouquet	–	calendar	3	challenge	8
brag	–	calorie	5	champion	3
braille	4	Canada	2	channel	5

chant	7	cling	9	constellation	5
chap	5	clink	–	constitute	–
chapel	–	closet	4	construct	7
chapter	3	clump	–	contagious	–
character	4	clumsy	2	contain	4
charcoal	3	cluster	–	continent	4
chariot	6	clutch	–	contrary	8
charm	3	coal	3	control	4
cheap	2	coarse	7	convenient	9
checkers	5	cobra	6	convince	4
chemical	3	cocoa	5	coop	–
chestnut	–	cod	7	cooperate	4
chill	–	coffee	4	cord	3
China	4	coffin	–	core	4
chip	K	coil	–	cork	K
chirp	4	coliseum	9	cot	–
choir	7	collect	3	cottage	4
choke	–	college	4	cottonwood	–
chord	4	collie	5	cougar	–
chore	5	colony	4	cough	5
chorus	4	comet	4	council	4
chow	–	comic	3	counter	4
chubby	–	comment	5	couple	6
chuck	3	commercial	4	coupon	6
chug	–	committee	5	courteous	7
cigar	–	communicate	4	courtyard	–
cinder	–	compass	3	cousin	3
cirrus	–	compose	–	coward	4
citizen	4	compound	7	coyote	4
clang	–	concentrate	4	cradle	5
clank	–	concert	5	crate	–
clarinet	8	condition	4	creak	5
clasp	–	congruent	3	create	5
clatter	–	conjunction	–	crew	7
click	10	consider	4	crib	6
climate	3	consist	6	crime	4

croak	4	definite	3	dizzy	4
crook	5	degree	4	dodo	11
crossword	4	den	4	dome	3
crouch	–	denomination	–	doodle	7
crowbar	–	dense	4	doubt	4
crumb	–	deny	7	dove	4
crunch	–	depend	4	downpour	6
crush	4	deposit	5	doze	11
crystal	8	depot	9	drab	9
cuckoo	–	deputy	11	drama	7
cuddle	–	deserve	12	drape	–
culture	5	desperate	5	drawbridge	–
cumulus	–	destroy	4	dribble	–
cupboard	5	detergent	11	drill	3
cure	3	detour	–	drizzle	10
current	4	Detroit	4	drought	5
custom	4	develop	4	duel	–
cycle	3	dew	6	duke	K
cylinder	3	diagram	3	dunce	7
cymbal	–	dial	5	dune	–
dab	4	diary	5	dung	–
dam	5	dice	5	dungeon	7
damage	4	diet	4	earthquake	3
dandy	–	dine	K	ease	7
dart	5	dioxide	3	echo	4
date	3	dip	4	educate	12
dawn	3	disappoint	9	effect	5
daze	6	disaster	5	effort	4
deadline	–	discipline	5	electron	4
deaf	3	discourage	9	elegant	4
death	5	discuss	7	element	4
deciduous	–	disguise	4	elk	–
decimal	5	displace	–	elsewhere	7
decrease	4	dissolve	5	embarrass	11
defend	5	ditch	4	emergency	7
define	4	divide	3	empire	7

England	4	fail	2	foreword	7
enlarge	4	faith	11	fort	6
enormous	2	fame	4	fortune	7
enthusiasm	4	fashion	4	foul	7
entire	4	fasten	4	fraction	3
envelope	4	favor	4	freckle	–
equal	3	fawn	–	freeway	9
equilateral	–	fee	5	freshman	7
error	4	ferry	6	fret	6
erupt	11	festival	5	friction	5
essay	6	fetch	–	frustrate	–
establish	5	file	4	fumble	–
estimate	3	film	5	fungus	5
evaporate	6	fin	5	furnace	4
event	4	finch	4	furnish	6
evidence	3	flannel	–	furniture	3
example	3	flare	11	further	8
excellent	5	flask	3	future	4
except	4	flavor	4	gallop	–
exchange	4	flea	8	gander	–
exercise	4	flesh	5	gang	5
exhale	–	fling	6	gangplank	–
exhaust	–	flip	–	gap	7
exhibit	4	flipper	–	garter	–
exist	4	flock	5	gauze	–
expect	5	flood	4	gear	5
expensive	4	fluff	–	general	4
experience	4	fluid	4	generous	4
expert	4	flute	3	genie	–
express	4	foam	11	geography	4
extend	7	folk	5	geranium	9
eyebrow	–	forbid	6	Germany	3
eyelash	–	ford	7	gigantic	6
factor	5	forearm	11	glacier	5
fade	–	forehead	–	glance	6
Fahrenheit	4	foreign	3	glare	5

glaze	–	grouch	–	hiccup	–
glimpse	4	grunt	5	hike	3
glisten	5	guide	3	hind	4
glitter	3	gulf	4	hinge	4
gloom	5	gully	6	hint	11
glossary	4	guppy	–	hiss	–
glow	5	gurgle	–	history	4
gnaw	4	gut	–	hitch	3
goal	6	guy	–	hobby	6
goblin	–	gym	5	hobo	4
goggles	7	gypsy	–	hockey	10
goldenrod	–	hail	5	hoe	5
golf	5	halo	–	holiday	3
gong	–	hammock	7	holler	–
gossip	–	handball	5	holly	–
grace	3	handcuff	–	holy	11
gradual	4	hardware	6	homespun	11
graduate	9	harmonica	9	homonym	–
gram	2	harpoon	–	hoof	–
grammar	7	Harrisburg	–	hoot	K
grasshopper	5	harrow	–	horizontal	7
grate	7	harsh	5	horror	5
grateful	4	Hartford	–	household	7
gravity	3	hatchet	2	however	4
graze	4	haul	5	hubbub	–
grease	5	hazard	5	huckleberry	–
Great Britain	–	hazel	–	huddle	4
greenhouse	1	headdress	–	humble	2
Greenland	4	headquarters	7	humid	5
greyhound	–	heal	5	hunch	9
griddle	–	health	3	hush	5
grill	5	heave	–	hutch	–
grind	4	heaven	–	hydrogen	4
grip	–	hedge	5	hymn	6
groan	3	hemisphere	5	hyphen	9
groom	3	hesitate	6	iceberg	7

icebox	–	janitor	5	latch	6
ideal	7	Japan	4	launch	4
idle	4	jaw	5	lava	4
igloo	–	jellyfish	5	lavender	–
ignite	10	jersey	4	layer	4
image	3	Jerusalem	7	leap	2
imagine	3	jewel	3	lease	10
imitate	9	jewelry	4	ledge	3
immediate	9	jig	5	legend	4
improve	5	journal	5	lens	5
increase	4	jug	7	lever	6
indent	–	juggle	–	liar	–
individual	5	junction	4	liberty	4
industry	5	junior	5	licorice	–
influence	4	junk	4	lily	6
inner	4	Jupiter	4	lime	3
inning	–	kernel	–	limestone	4
innocent	4	kettle	5	limp	4
insist	4	keyboard	–	lipstick	–
inspect	–	kid	4	litter	2
instant	5	kidney	–	liver	7
instruct	6	kimono	–	llama	4
intelligent	5	knit	–	loan	3
interrupt	4	knothole	–	lobby	9
intestine	7	knuckle	7	locate	1
introduce	7	lab	9	locket	4
invent	5	labor	7	lodge	8
invisible	4	laboratory	7	London	3
inward	6	lack	4	loom	9
iodine	9	ladle	–	lope	7
irrigate	6	lame	–	lord	5
itch	4	lantern	7	loss	5
jabber	–	lariat	–	lotion	8
jack	1	lark	–	luggage	7
jackknife	–	lash	–	lumber	3
Jacksonville	5	lass	–	lunar	7

lurch	–	Mercury	4	muscle	7
macaroni	–	mermaid	4	mustache	7
magma	11	mesa	7	mustard	3
magnificent	5	meteor	4	mutt	–
magnify	7	metric	4	myth	5
maintain	5	Mexico	4	nab	–
manage	4	midnight	3	naked	6
mane	4	Milwaukee	9	napkin	–
mantle	4	minnow	–	nasty	7
manufacture	6	minor	3	native	4
manure	–	mission	4	nature	3
maple	3	mister	–	naughty	–
marble	4	mitt	3	navy	4
marigold	7	mittens	–	necessary	5
marmalade	10	moccasin	12	Neptune	6
Mars	4	mock	–	Netherlands	10
mascot	5	model	4	neutron	4
mash	4	moderate	9	New Orleans	–
mast	5	moist	4	nibble	5
master	–	mollusk	4	nightmare	–
material	4	monitor	4	nitrogen	3
math	4	mood	5	nook	9
mattress	–	mop	3	nor	5
maypole	–	Moscow	7	Norway	7
McKinley	–	motion	4	notch	5
meanwhile	6	mount	–	novel	5
mechanic	4	movie	1	nozzle	–
medium	7	muff	–	nucleus	4
melody	–	muffin	–	nudge	–
melon	3	muffler	–	numb	4
memorial	8	mug	–	nun	–
memory	4	muggy	–	nuzzle	–
Memphis	5	multiply	3	nylon	8
mend	6	mumble	4	oar	9
mental	7	mummy	5	oasis	4
menu	5	munch	–	oats	7

oblong	4	participate	5	pill	4
oboe	–	particular	5	pillar	–
observe	4	partner	4	pinch	9
occupation	5	passenger	4	pineapple	–
occur	6	patent	9	pinwheel	–
Omaha	5	patient	4	pistol	6
omit	4	patio	9	pit	3
ooze	–	patrol	4	pity	4
operate	4	pause	4	pixy	–
opportunity	5	pave	–	planetarium	4
orchestra	5	peace	4	plaster	11
ordinary	6	peak	3	plateau	4
organ	12	pearl	5	platform	3
organize	5	pebble	4	platter	5
orient	–	peck	7	plaza	4
oriole	–	peer	5	plop	–
ornament	5	pelican	12	plot	6
ornery	–	penetrate	4	plum	3
ostrich	7	pennant	–	plumber	5
ounce	4	percussion	–	plump	5
outfit	5	perennial	7	plural	6
outskirts	–	perfume	9	Pluto	5
overalls	4	permit	4	pod	5
owe	7	Persia	4	poet	5
pad	4	petticoat	–	poison	4
padlock	4	petunia	–	policy	5
pantry	–	pheasant	8	polish	4
papoose	–	Philadelphia	5	polka	12
parable	–	Phoenix	4	poll	4
parachute	9	phonograph	5	pollute	4
paraffin	7	photosynthesis	5	polygon	–
paragraph	3	phrase	3	poncho	–
parallelogram	6	piccolo	–	poodle	6
parcel	6	pickle	5	popover	–
pardon	–	pickup	4	popular	3
parenthesis	–	pigtail	–	porcupine	7

porpoise	5	Providence	–	realize	5
porridge	–	prowl	5	receipt	2
port	3	public	3	receive	4
portfolio	9	publish	5	recipe	4
position	5	pulley	–	recognize	5
positive	4	pullover	–	recover	6
postage	7	pulse	3	redcoat	–
postmaster	–	punch	4	reduce	4
postpone	–	punctuate	–	redwood	11
posture	7	puncture	4	reed	6
poultry	4	pupa	3	regard	7
practical	6	purpose	3	region	4
prairie	4	putter	–	regret	7
preach	6	pyramid	4	rein	–
precious	4	quadrilateral	–	rely	6
precipitation	5	quail	10	remark	4
predicate	4	qualify	6	repeat	7
prefer	4	quarantine	5	represent	4
prefix	4	quarrel	4	rescue	3
preposition	–	quartet	–	research	6
prevent	3	quilt	5	reservoir	7
pride	7	quiver	4	respond	5
primary	5	quotient	–	responsible	4
principal	4	raccoon	2	result	4
prism	5	racket	5	reveal	5
prison	5	raft	5	revoke	–
private	5	rage	5	revolution	4
process	4	rail	–	Richmond	–
procrastinate	–	railway	7	ridge	11
product	4	ramp	7	rifle	6
program	3	rapid	5	rigid	7
proof	4	rattle	5	rinse	–
proofread	–	rattlesnake	4	rise	3
property	5	raw	5	rot	4
proton	4	ray	K	rough	3
protrude	11	razor	9	route	4

routine	6	scum	–	sierra	8
royal	4	seafood	6	sift	5
ruby	2	seam	K	silverware	–
ruff	–	Seattle	8	similar	4
ruffle	–	seaweed	5	simile	11
runaway	–	secretary	4	siren	10
rung	4	secrete	–	sissy	–
runt	–	secure	5	situation	6
rural	4	seek	4	skein	–
Russia	4	seldom	5	skid	7
rust	4	senior	4	skillet	–
rustle	5	sensitive	6	skim	11
rustler	–	series	4	skinny	7
sag	–	sermon	–	skittish	–
Sahara	4	sewer	11	slab	–
sake	11	sex	5	slacks	7
salary	4	shack	–	slam	3
salmon	4	shale	4	slang	–
San Diego	–	shallow	4	slant	10
sandal	–	shame	8	slash	4
sash	–	shampoo	4	sleet	6
satellite	4	shawl	5	slender	4
Saturn	4	sherbet	6	slick	7
sawmill	–	shift	–	slight	4
saxophone	–	shipment	2	slim	4
scalp	–	shortening	4	sling	–
scene	4	shorthand	–	slip	4
scent	–	shortstop	4	slop	–
scoot	–	shoulders	5	slug	–
scout	4	shred	5	sly	4
scowl	2	shrill	9	smack	–
scramble	–	shrub	4	smear	–
screw	9	shrug	–	smith	3
screwdriver	6	shuffle	–	smog	7
scrimp	12	sideburns	–	smokestack	–
scripture	–	sideways	7	smother	4

smudge	–	spat	–	stall	5
snail	3	spatula	–	stallion	–
snapdragon	–	spear	5	staple	7
sneak	3	species	7	startle	4
snicker	–	speck	4	steadfast	–
snip	–	spectacles	–	steady	4
snoop	–	sphere	4	steak	4
snooze	–	spice	11	steel	3
snore	–	spike	–	steep	4
snort	–	spinach	3	steeple	–
snub	–	spiral	5	sting	4
snug	–	spit	–	stingy	9
sober	7	splice	–	stink	–
soccer	5	splinter	–	stitch	3
social	2	sponge	4	stock	2
sofa	7	sponsor	9	stockade	–
softball	6	spook	–	stopwatch	–
soggy	7	spore	12	strain	5
solar	4	sport	3	strait	6
solid	3	sprain	–	streak	8
solo	8	spread	K	stretch	3
solve	3	sprout	5	strict	11
somersault	–	spur	7	stride	–
somewhat	5	sputter	–	stroke	5
sonar	–	squash	8	stroll	8
soothe	5	squat	5	structure	6
sore	4	squaw	–	struggle	7
source	5	squirm	–	strum	–
souvenir	–	squirt	5	stubborn	5
soybean	–	St. Louis	–	stumble	–
spa	–	staff	4	stump	5
spaghetti	3	stage	3	sturdy	2
Spain	4	stagecoach	4	subject	4
spangle	–	stain	7	submarine	3
spaniel	–	stale	–	subway	2
sparrow	9	stalk	–	succeed	4

suck	7	tassel	–	tiddlywinks	–
suffer	–	taupe	–	tide	4
sufficient	5	tee	5	tilt	–
suffix	4	teenager	6	timid	7
suggest	5	teepee	9	tingle	–
suitcase	5	teeter	–	tinsel	–
sum	4	telegram	9	tint	7
sunflower	5	telegraph	4	tiresome	–
super	4	telescope	7	'tis	–
superior	5	telltale	–	toadstool	10
supply	5	temper	–	Tokyo	5
support	4	temple	3	tole	–
suppose	4	tend	7	tom-tom	–
surround	4	tennis	3	tomahawk	–
suspect	5	termite	4	tomboy	–
suspender	5	terrier	–	tone	2
swamp	7	territory	4	tong	–
swan	–	text	7	toot	–
sway	5	texture	–	topic	4
swear	–	thaw	4	torch	–
sweat	–	thee	–	total	5
swell	4	theft	7	tough	3
swift	4	therefore	4	tow	6
syllable	4	thimble	–	trademark	–
synonym	4	thistle	–	tramp	–
synthesis	8	thong	–	trampoline	9
tab	–	thorax	–	trapeze	6
tablet	–	thorn	9	treble	–
tack	4	thou	–	tricycle	5
tackle	4	thrill	4	trim	5
talent	6	thud	5	trinket	–
tambourine	–	thumbtack	–	trio	–
tame	3	thump	5	trombone	3
tank	3	thus	6	troop	3
tardy	2	thy	4	trophy	4

trousers	–	vein	9	wham	–
trundle	–	Venus	4	wharf	4
truth	2	veranda	–	wheelchair	–
tuba	8	vessel	5	whiff	10
tuck	6	veterinarian	–	whine	9
tumble	3	vibrate	5	whinny	4
turnip	6	video	9	whirl	4
twine	–	view	4	wick	–
twinkle	5	vine	4	wicker	–
twirl	–	vinegar	4	widow	4
typewrite	–	violet	7	wigwam	–
umpire	5	vocabulary	K	wildcat	–
unicorn	6	volcano	4	wilderness	6
uniform	5	volume	4	windpipe	10
union	4	vote	3	wizard	9
universe	3	vulture	7	workout	–
upland	–	waddle	–	worship	5
upright	5	wade	5	wreath	–
Uranus	6	walrus	5	wrestle	–
urgent	2	waltz	–	wrinkle	4
Uruguay	–	wasp	4	xylophone	–
vampire	7	wax	3	yak	–
vapor	4	wealth	5	yap	8
vary	7	weasel	–	Yellowstone	5
vase	5	web	5	youth	5
vegetation	7	wedge	6	zero	7
vehicle	9	wee	9	zone	3
veil	–	whack	–		

FIFTH GRADE

abandon	4	alkaline	7	archery	5
Abilene	–	allegiance	–	arena	6
aborigine	–	alloy	7	Argentina	5
abroad	7	almond	–	armor	5
absolute	6	Alps	5	armpit	–
abuse	5	altar	11	aroma	–
access	8	alto	–	array	–
accessory	7	ambassador	5	artery	9
accompany	5	amber	–	asbestos	–
accomplish	5	ambition	6	asparagus	6
account	5	amble	9	assemble	7
accurate	5	ammonia	–	assist	7
acre	7	ammunition	5	assume	7
adapt	5	amphibian	5	assure	–
adequate	5	analyze	5	asteroid	5
administer	–	ancestor	5	astonish	7
admiral	6	angle	5	astronaut	5
adobe	12	anteater	7	astronomy	9
advance	7	antenna	5	attain	–
advantage	5	antibiotics	9	attempt	5
advertise	5	anticipate	5	attire	11
advise	6	antidote	4	attorney	6
Aegean	–	antique	5	Austin	4
affect	5	antler	7	Austria	7
affection	7	Appalachian	9	authority	5
afterward	7	appeal	7	automatic	11
agent	5	appliance	9	auxiliary	–
aircraft	5	apply	K	available	5
airfield	–	appoint	6	avalanche	5
airman	–	appropriate	7	aviator	5
airstrip	–	apt	6	avocado	11
ajar	8	aqueduct	–	awning	–
Albany	5	arbor	–	axis	6
alcohol	5	arc	6	azure	–
algebra	12	arcade	7	bacteria	5

badger	–	bleak	–	broth	–
badminton	–	blindfold	4	browse	6
bagpipe	–	blister	–	brunette	–
bail	6	blockade	9	Brussels	–
bait	4	blockhead	–	brute	–
balsa	8	blockhouse	–	buck	8
Baltimore	6	blonde	–	buckskin	–
ban	2	bloodhound	–	buff	11
bangle	–	blubber	–	bugle	–
banister	–	bluebell	–	bulge	10
barber	7	bluff	10	bulk	–
bareback	8	blunder	–	bulldoze	–
barometer	7	blunt	5	burr	–
baseboard	–	blur	–	bustle	–
bashful	5	bob	1	butt	9
bass	7	bog	–	butterscotch	–
basswood	–	bologna	7	cabinet	2
beacon	6	bonfire	5	cackle	–
bedrock	–	bonny	–	cad	3
beech	–	boom	5	cafe	5
beeline	–	boomerang	–	cafeteria	5
Beijing	7	bosom	–	caffeine	9
belle	–	boxwood	–	calcium	5
bellhop	–	brace	2	calculate	7
bellow	–	bravo	7	calico	5
beret	10	Brazil	5	camel	4
berth	–	breathtaking	8	campus	5
beta	7	breed	10	canal	5
betray	–	briar	–	cancer	7
billfold	–	bridle	6	candidate	5
bind	6	bristle	–	cannibal	7
binoculars	12	Britain	5	cannon	–
biology	7	brittle	–	canopy	10
birthmark	–	broil	–	canteen	–
biscuit	–	bronco	–	canvas	4
bishop	–	brood	K	caravan	4

cardigan	–	chlorine	9	cockroach	–
cargo	4	chlorophyll	5	coconut	3
Caribbean	5	chopsticks	4	coke	9
carousel	–	chowder	7	coleslaw	9
carp	–	chrome	5	coliseum	–
cartilage	–	chrysanthemum	–	collapse	5
cartridge	7	chum	–	cologne	–
cashew	–	chute	5	colon	–
cask	–	cider	–	combat	5
casual	–	cinch	–	combine	9
catalogue	–	Cincinnati	5	comedy	7
catastrophe	–	cinnamon	5	commerce	7
cavalry	11	circuit	6	commonplace	–
cease	–	circumference	7	commotion	5
celestial	5	cistern	–	companion	6
cellulose	7	citrus	–	compare	4
census	5	civil	5	compartment	7
ceramic	11	clad	–	compel	–
ceremony	4	claim	5	compete	5
chafe	–	clamor	7	competent	4
chairman	–	clamp	–	complex	7
chalet	–	clan	5	complexion	–
chamber	7	clash	–	complicate	10
chandelier	6	clause	11	compliment	5
chaps	–	clench	–	comprehend	9
charity	6	Cleveland	5	compute	11
charter	7	clinic	9	concave	11
chat	5	cloak	5	conceal	6
checkmate	–	clockwork	–	concern	5
chef	6	clog	7	conclude	11
chemistry	5	clot	–	concrete	6
chess	8	clothespin	–	condense	9
Cheyenne	–	clutter	8	confess	8
chime	K	coax	–	confetti	–
chinaware	–	cobblestone	8	confident	5
chisel	2	cockpit	–	confirm	6

conflict	5	crane	K	damn	–
confuse	7	crater	5	dandruff	7
congratulate	–	crave	8	dangle	9
congress	5	crayfish	5	dapple	–
connect	7	crease	4	darling	–
conquer	6	credit	7	data	5
conscious	5	crescendo	–	dazzle	–
conserve	7	crescent	7	debt	4
considerate	6	crest	–	decay	5
consistent	7	cringe	–	decent	9
constant	5	crochet	7	deckhand	4
constitution	5	crock	–	declare	6
consult	5	crotch	–	decline	4
contact	5	croup	–	decoy	6
contract	5	cruise	5	dedicate	6
contrast	7	crumble	4	deed	11
contrite	–	crumple	–	defeat	5
convention	6	crutch	–	deflate	–
convex	11	cubbyhole	–	defrost	5
convict	–	cubic	5	delay	5
cookout	5	cue	7	delicate	4
cornet	–	cuff	–	delta	5
cornucopia	–	cultivate	9	demand	5
corridor	–	culvert	–	democracy	7
corrugate	–	cuneiform	–	demolish	–
corsage	–	curb	–	demon	7
cosmetics	8	curd	–	demonstrate	9
cottontail	–	curriculum	–	denim	9
couch	5	curse	9	Denmark	–
counsel	–	cushion	4	dentistry	7
counterfeit	9	custody	–	depart	9
cove	–	cuticle	–	depress	9
covey	–	cutlass	–	descend	5
cowslip	–	cyclone	–	destiny	–
coy	–	dagger	–	detect	7
crag	–	dame	–	determine	6

device	5	dominant	9	economics	5
devour	–	donate	7	edible	6
diagnose	5	doom	5	eel	5
diagonal	–	dope	–	eerie	–
dialect	–	downfall	9	efficient	4
diameter	6	draft	5	Egypt	5
diaphragm	–	dragonfly	–	elect	5
differ	5	drake	7	embankment	–
digest	6	drawl	–	emblem	10
dignity	7	dreary	6	embrace	–
dike	–	drench	5	embroider	–
diminish	11	droop	–	emerald	6
dingo	–	dry goods	–	emphasis	9
diploma	–	duchess	–	employ	6
discount	6	duct	7	encourage	5
disease	4	dude	–	enrich	4
disgrace	9	due	6	environment	4
disk	–	duet	–	envy	5
dismal	4	dugout	–	epidemic	4
dismiss	8	dumbbell	–	episode	6
dispatch	9	dungarees	–	equation	7
display	6	durable	5	equip	–
dispose	4	dusk	–	essence	–
dispute	4	duty	5	essential	7
distinct	4	dwindle	–	eternity	9
distinguish	12	dye	5	Ethiopia	–
distress	10	dynamite	9	eventual	–
divorce	–	earl	7	exaggerate	9
document	7	earnest	9	exceed	9
doe	–	earphone	–	excel	10
dogie	–	earshot	–	excess	5
dogwood	–	easel	–	expedition	5
doily	–	eaves	–	explode	–
dolphin	5	ebb	–	exponent	–
dolt	–	eclipse	6	export	5
domestic	7	ecology	11	expose	6

exterior	5	flapjack	–	frail	4
extinct	5	flatter	–	frantic	5
extinguish	10	flaw	9	fraternity	–
eyepiece	–	flax	–	fray	11
fable	11	fleece	7	freak	–
fabric	8	flex	–	freight	6
fabulous	3	flick	–	frequent	5
fad	8	flimsy	–	frill	–
falter	–	flint	7	fringe	6
fang	–	flora	12	frolic	–
fantastic	5	floss	–	frontier	5
fare	5	flounder	–	fume	6
farewell	7	flue	–	function	6
fatal	6	fluke	–	fund	5
fate	6	fluorescent	7	funnel	6
fathom	4	focus	7	furl	–
feature	6	foe	6	fury	–
federal	5	fond	7	fuss	–
fend	–	foothill	10	gag	5
fender	9	fore	–	gain	5
ferment	5	forecast	6	galaxy	6
ferret	5	foreman	–	gale	5
fertile	6	forge	10	gallant	–
fertilize	–	forklift	–	gape	–
fever	7	forlorn	–	gardenia	–
fiber	–	formal	5	gargle	–
fiddle	–	former	6	garland	–
fidget	–	formula	4	garlic	7
fig	–	fortress	11	garrison	–
figurehead	–	foster	5	gauge	5
filter	5	foundation	5	gazelle	–
filth	5	fourscore	–	gee	7
firearms	–	foxglove	–	gel	–
fizz	–	fracas	–	gem	5
flair	–	fragment	4	generate	9
Flanders	–	fragrant	6	genius	6

genuine	9	grumble	4	hitchhike	–
geology	12	guilt	7	hoarse	5
geometry	11	gush	–	hobble	–
Gettysburg	5	gust	4	hog	–
geyser	–	gutter	4	hogan	–
ghetto	–	guzzle	–	hoist	5
glade	–	habitat	–	homely	–
gland	–	halt	2	homestead	8
gleam	2	halter	–	honeydew	–
glee	–	hamper	–	honeymoon	–
glory	9	handicap	8	honeysuckle	–
gloss	–	hare	8	hopper	–
gnash	10	hark	–	horde	–
gob	–	harness	–	horizon	5
gorge	6	haste	5	hornet	9
govern	6	haunt	7	horsepower	5
grandstand	6	haven	12	hostile	7
granite	5	haze	5	hourglass	–
grasp	6	headset	5	howdy	–
gratitude	6	headstone	–	hue	7
grave	–	hearth	7	hummingbird	–
gravel	5	heathen	–	hump	11
Greece	5	hectic	9	humus	–
grenade	–	hedgehog	–	hurricane	4
grief	5	heir	–	husk	–
grim	6	heirloom	8	hydroelectric	11
grime	8	helter-skelter	–	hypothesis	7
grit	–	hereby	–	identity	5
groggy	–	herewith	–	ignorant	6
groove	–	heroine	–	ignore	4
grope	–	heron	7	illegal	11
gross	9	herring	5	illustrate	9
grout	–	hexagon	–	immune	–
grove	6	hickory	–	imp	3
grub	–	highness	–	implement	7
gruff	7	hilarious	9	import	5

impress	7	invert	–	lacrosse	–
impulse	9	invest	9	lag	2
incense	6	investigate	6	lair	–
incident	5	invoice	–	landlord	4
incline	11	involve	5	landmark	8
include	7	ion	7	lapse	–
income	5	Iran	7	larkspur	–
independent	5	irritate	9	latex	–
India	4	Israel	9	lather	–
infant	6	issue	5	latitude	6
infantry	–	jab	–	latter	–
infect	–	jackass	–	lattice	5
inferior	6	jailbird	–	laurel	4
inform	7	jealous	5	league	6
informal	5	jest	5	leash	5
inhabit	–	jiffy	–	lecture	8
inhale	–	jitter	–	legal	6
initial	4	jog	5	lend	4
injure	6	johnnycake	–	lest	–
inland	5	jot	–	Lexington	5
inlet	–	jumbo	–	license	7
input	11	juvenile	4	linen	5
inquire	–	katydid	5	liner	–
insert	8	kayak	11	linger	7
inspire	8	keen	7	link	7
install	6	keg	–	linoleum	–
instinct	6	kelp	–	lisp	–
insult	7	kerchief	–	literature	5
integer	–	khaki	7	litmus	5
intense	6	kidnap	10	livelihood	5
intent	7	kiln	–	loam	–
interior	5	kinetic	5	lob	–
intermediate	11	knack	–	lobe	9
interpret	6	knead	–	local	5
intersect	6	knight	6	locomotive	3
interview	5	knob	5	locust	6

loft	11	mason	5	mole	6
longitude	6	masquerade	6	molecule	5
loot	–	mass	4	molt	–
lottery	6	mature	9	monarch	12
Louisville	5	mayonnaise	–	monastery	–
lounge	–	meditate	–	Montgomery	5
loyal	4	Mediterranean	4	monument	7
lozenge	–	medley	11	moreover	5
lumberjack	5	meek	5	mortal	–
lung	–	mellow	5	mortgage	4
lunge	–	merchant	7	motto	7
luxury	9	mercy	4	mourn	5
lye	–	merit	4	mucus	5
lyric	–	midst	11	multitude	6
magenta	–	midway	8	municipal	7
mainland	10	migrate	4	mural	6
mainstay	–	mildew	–	murder	11
maize	–	military	5	murky	–
majesty	–	millipede	–	murmur	–
mallard	–	mimic	8	muskrat	7
malt	3	mineral	5	mustang	–
mammoth	5	miniature	10	muster	–
manganese	–	minister	5	mute	–
manicure	–	mink	–	muzzle	–
manor	7	minority	8	nag	–
mansion	7	minuet	–	naval	5
mantel	–	miracle	4	navigate	6
manual	7	mischief	–	nectar	5
mar	9	missile	5	negative	2
mare	7	mistress	–	neigh	–
marine	6	mite	–	neon	5
marionette	12	mob	9	network	9
maroon	7	mockingbird	–	neutral	7
marsh	9	modify	8	nevertheless	7
marvelous	6	module	–	Niagara	–
masculine	9	molasses	7	nicknack	–

Nigeria	5	ornate	9	parliament	5
nigh	11	orphan	–	parlor	–
nightfall	7	otherwise	6	parole	–
Nile	5	outcome	7	participle	9
noble	9	outlaw	6	pastel	9
nominate	–	outlet	6	pasteurize	–
normal	5	outline	5	pastime	9
nostril	–	outpost	–	pastor	–
notify	7	outsmart	–	pastry	7
nourish	–	outstanding	5	patty	–
nuclear	6	outward	6	payroll	9
nude	–	ovary	7	peal	–
nugget	–	overboard	–	peat	–
null	–	overcast	7	pecan	–
obsidian	–	overcome	5	peculiar	7
obstacle	6	overlook	5	peg	1
obstruct	–	overwhelm	7	pellet	9
obtain	6	oxide	7	pelt	10
obvious	5	oyster	8	penalty	11
occasion	5	pace	6	penicillin	4
occupy	4	paddy	–	peninsula	11
octagon	–	Pakistan	–	penmanship	8
octave	–	palette	–	pentagon	6
octopus	5	pamphlet	5	pep	–
offend	–	panel	6	per	4
official	5	panic	8	percent	5
offset	–	panorama	–	perform	3
offshore	–	panther	6	perish	6
ointment	9	paperback	5	permanent	5
Olympic	5	parakeet	9	perpendicular	5
omelet	5	parallel	5	personal	5
opal	–	paralyze	–	perspire	–
opera	8	parasite	7	Peru	6
opossum	–	parasol	–	petroleum	6
opponent	5	parchment	–	phantom	–
origin	5	Paris	5	pharmacy	6

photograph	6	Portugal	5	promote	7
physical	5	posh	–	prop	–
physician	5	posse	–	propel	5
pierce	5	potion	–	prophet	–
pigment	–	Potomac	–	prospector	8
pimple	–	pouch	5	protein	4
pinafore	–	pounce	–	proverb	11
pinball	7	pout	5	province	–
ping	5	poverty	3	prune	–
pinto	5	powder	5	pry	–
pitchfork	–	powwow	–	pucker	–
pith	–	precise	6	pudgy	–
Pittsburgh	5	pregnant	11	pueblo	4
plague	–	premium	–	pug	–
plaid	–	preserve	5	pulpit	–
plank	–	previous	6	puma	–
plaque	5	prey	5	pumice	–
platypus	7	price	3	pun	9
pliers	6	prick	–	puny	–
plod	–	priest	5	purchase	4
plume	–	prime	6	puritan	8
plunder	9	primer	–	pursue	5
plunge	9	primitive	7	putty	–
plunk	–	principle	7	pygmy	–
plywood	–	privilege	9	quaint	9
poach	–	pro	7	quality	4
poker	–	probable	5	quantity	8
Poland	5	probe	11	quarterback	5
polio	–	proceed	–	quartz	11
politics	5	procession	5	Quebec	3
polo	6	profession	5	quill	5
pompom	–	profile	–	quirk	–
pope	–	profit	4	rabies	–
porcelain	6	project	4	radiate	–
pore	9	projector	6	radium	–
portion	8	promenade	–	radius	5

ragweed	–	reserve	8	runway	5
raid	7	resin	–	rustic	–
ramshackle	7	resist	6	Sacramento	9
rank	5	resort	6	sacred	5
rap	5	resource	3	saint	6
rapids	11	restore	4	Salem	3
rascal	–	retina	–	saliva	5
rash	7	reverse	7	salon	9
rate	4	revise	–	saloon	8
raven	–	revolt	5	Salt Lake City	–
ravine	6	revolver	–	salute	6
reap	4	rickety	7	sandpaper	7
rebel	5	ridicule	–	saucy	–
recent	5	rim	7	savage	6
reckless	5	rind	–	scab	–
recommend	6	risk	4	scamp	–
recorder	6	rival	5	scan	8
recreation	6	roan	–	scarce	5
recycle	7	role	5	scarlet	6
reek	–	Rome	5	scheme	5
refer	4	romp	5	scholar	–
reflect	4	rookie	–	scoff	–
regal	9	roost	6	scorch	8
register	6	roster	–	scorn	11
rehearse	2	rotate	6	Scotland	5
reign	7	rouge	7	scourge	–
rejoice	9	rubbish	4	scrap	6
relay	4	rubble	11	scrawl	–
release	7	ruckus	–	scrawny	–
relish	5	rudder	5	screech	–
render	–	ruddy	–	script	5
repel	5	rugged	6	scuffle	–
republic	5	rumble	11	scurvy	–
require	5	rumor	–	sediment	5
resemble	4	rump	–	seep	–
resent	11	rumpus	–	segment	5

semester	7	skull	5	sorrow	5
senate	5	skyline	–	spatter	–
senior	5	slack	–	spearmint	–
serene	7	slat	–	sperm	9
session	8	slate	4	sphinx	–
severe	5	slaughter	7	spine	6
shaft	–	slay	–	spinster	–
shamble	–	slingshot	–	spire	7
shank	–	slink	–	spirit	5
shark	5	slit	–	splendid	9
shatter	7	sliver	–	spool	11
sheaf	–	slogan	6	spout	–
shear	11	slope	5	sprawl	5
sheath	7	slosh	–	sprig	–
shield	6	slot	2	Springfield	–
shilling	–	slum	11	sprint	6
shimmer	–	slump	8	spruce	–
shin	2	slush	6	spurt	12
shingle	5	smelt	–	squadron	–
showdown	–	smirk	–	squall	–
shriek	6	smug	–	squelch	–
shrivel	–	snapper	5	squint	5
shudder	7	snapshot	–	stab	–
shun	–	snare	5	stadium	5
sieve	9	snarl	–	stag	–
silicon	–	sneer	–	stagger	–
silkworm	–	snorkel	–	stake	5
silt	6	snout	5	stamina	7
sincere	5	snuggle	4	stammer	–
singe	–	society	6	stampede	6
sire	–	sod	–	stanza	–
site	6	sodium	9	starboard	–
sketch	10	sole	2	starch	4
skipper	4	solemn	7	stateroom	–
skirmish	–	solution	6	static	5
skit	6	somber	7	stead	–

stereo	8	sulk	–	temperate	6
sterile	11	sultan	–	tempest	–
stern	–	summary	9	tempo	–
stile	–	summit	6	temporary	6
stilt	–	sundial	–	tempt	5
stimulate	9	superb	10	tense	5
stingray	–	superlative	11	term	4
stirrup	6	supernatural	6	terminal	6
stoke	–	superstition	6	terrain	4
stomp	–	supreme	5	terrific	7
stoop	9	surf	7	terry	6
strangle	–	surgery	7	testament	–
strategy	6	survey	5	testimony	–
stratosphere	9	survive	5	textile	7
stray	7	swagger	–	thatch	6
streetcar	–	swap	–	theater	5
stress	5	swarm	8	theme	5
strife	11	swash	–	theory	7
strut	–	swoop	–	thermal	6
stub	7	swordfish	–	thicket	–
stud	–	symmetry	5	thigh	–
studio	5	sympathy	7	thrash	–
stun	–	symptom	7	threat	5
stunt	5	taffy	–	thresh	–
stutter	–	tang	12	thrive	11
style	5	tangerine	–	throb	7
submerge	5	tangle	–	throng	–
subscribe	–	tar	7	thunderbolt	–
subsist	–	target	4	thunderhead	–
suburb	5	tariff	–	tidings	–
suds	–	tart	7	tidy	–
suede	–	tatter	11	tile	5
suicide	–	tawny	–	timber	6
suite	10	tax	4	tinderbox	–
suitor	–	teat	–	tinge	10
sulfur	7	technology	5	tinkle	–

tissue	5	trumpet	5	vanilla	6
tobacco	7	tuber	–	vanish	5
toffee	–	tuft	–	variety	6
toil	–	tugboat	–	varnish	–
toll	2	tumor	11	vast	5
tomb	5	tuna	5	vat	5
tornado	4	tundra	7	vault	–
torpedo	6	turban	–	Venezuela	–
tortilla	–	turf	7	vengeance	–
tot	6	turnout	–	Venice	5
totem	5	turquoise	5	vent	–
tour	3	twain	5	ventriloquist	–
tradition	5	twang	–	verge	–
transistor	–	tweezers	–	verify	9
translate	4	twitch	4	vermilion	–
transplant	11	udder	–	verse	6
transport	5	underbrush	–	vertebrate	5
trapezoid	–	underdog	–	vertical	5
treaty	6	undergo	10	Vesuvius	–
tremendous	6	undergrowth	–	victim	5
trench	5	underworld	8	vigor	–
trespass	9	unicycle	7	vineyard	–
tributary	8	unite	9	viola	–
tribute	–	university	6	violent	6
trice	–	unravel	–	virgin	–
trigger	–	upholster	–	virus	9
trill	–	uproar	6	visible	7
trillion	–	uranium	6	vision	5
triple	9	urban	5	visor	–
triumph	–	urge	4	vital	7
trooper	–	usher	7	vitamin	4
tropics	6	vaccine	–	vivid	10
trough	5	vacuum	11	void	11
troupe	11	vain	5	volley	–
trout	5	Vancouver	–	vow	–
trudge	4	vandal	–	wad	–

wallet	4	whist	–	yacht	–
wallflower	–	whittle	5	yank	–
walnut	–	whop	–	yearling	–
wand	–	wield	–	yelp	–
wardrobe	–	wine	4	yield	1
warehouse	5	wit	7	yip	–
warp	9	withdraw	5	yodel	5
wart	–	wither	5	yonder	–
waylay	–	withstand	–	Yosemite	–
weapon	5	witness	2	youngster	9
weave	9	wobble	–	yowl	–
weird	7	woodchuck	–	Yugoslavia	5
werewolf	7	woodwind	5	Yukon	–
wheeze	–	workshop	6	zigzag	7
whereas	9	wren	7	zinc	6
whiplash	–	wring	–		

SIXTH GRADE

abbot	–	alien	9	assault	7
abduct	10	Allegheny	–	associate	–
abreast	–	ally	9	astrology	9
abrupt	7	alpha	7	Athens	5
abscess	–	alter	6	attribute	–
abstain	–	alternate	6	auction	6
abstract	7	amateur	–	audio	–
absurd	6	Amazon	7	audition	–
abundant	6	ambiguous	–	authentic	6
academy	9	amethyst	–	avail	–
accelerate	–	amnesia	9	aviation	9
accommodate	–	ample	6	Babylon	6
accord	–	Amsterdam	–	bachelor	6
achieve	5	amuck	–	backfire	–
acknowledge	9	analogy	–	backhand	–
acquaint	7	anemone	9	Baghdad	–
acquire	9	animate	9	balk	–
acropolis	–	anonymous	–	ballot	7
acute	6	anthracite	–	bandanna	
adept	–	antic	–	barb	–
adhesive	7	apostle	–	barge	6
Adirondacks	–	appall	–	barley	7
adjacent	6	apparatus	12	baron	–
adore	8	apparel	10	barracks	7
aerial	–	apparent	5	barren	6
affix	4	appendix	7	barricade	7
afflict	–	apprentice	6	barrier	6
aggregate	–	aqua	–	basis	6
agile	7	Arabia	5	baste	11
airborne	–	arachnid	6	bauxite	7
airway	–	arid	11	bazaar	6
alas	–	arsenal	–	bearing	11
albatross	10	arson	–	beckon	6
Alexandria	–	ascend	6	bedlam	7
Algeria	–	asphalt	7	beforehand	9

behalf	–	boon	–	calamity	7
Belgium	5	Bosporus	–	calligraphy	–
Belgrade	–	boulevard	7	Cambodia	–
benefit	5	bounds	–	Cambridge	5
beriberi	–	bowel	–	camouflage	8
Berlin	5	boycott	6	campaign	5
beryllium	6	bracket	–	Canterbury	–
beset	–	brainstorm	–	caption	–
bestow	–	bran	9	captive	–
beverage	3	brawn	–	Caracas	–
bevy	–	bray	–	carbonate	–
bias	–	breadwinner	–	carcass	–
biceps	–	breakwater	–	caress	–
bicuspid	–	bribe	–	Carthage	–
billboard	–	brigade	–	cascade	11
bin	–	brink	7	caste	–
binary	–	broadcast	5	category	7
bisect	–	broadside	–	cathedral	7
bison	9	broker	6	causeway	–
bizarre	11	bromine	–	Ceylon	–
blab	–	Bronx	–	champagne	–
blackhead	–	Brooklyn	4	Charleston	5
blacktop	6	Brownsville	–	Charlotte	7
blare	–	Bulgaria	–	chasm	–
bleach	–	bumble	–	chaste	–
blemish	–	bungalow	–	chauffeur	–
blight	–	bungle	–	Chesapeake	–
blimp	–	bunker	–	Chile	6
boarder	7	bunt	–	Chinook	–
bobcat	8	burden	11	chivalry	–
Bohemia	–	bureau	9	cholesterol	9
Bolivia	6	burly	–	chromatic	–
bolt	9	Burma	–	chronology	–
bonbon	–	busboy	–	cigarette	–
bond	6	byway	–	cinema	–
bondage	7	Cairo	5	circumstance	9

civic	–	conform	11	creed	–
clapboard	–	confound	–	Crete	–
clarify	11	congest	–	crevice	–
clarity	9	conglomerate	5	crimson	7
classic	9	conquest	5	crinkle	–
cleft	–	conscience	7	cripple	–
clerk	6	consecutive	8	crisis	6
client	10	consent	10	crisscross	–
climax	8	consequence	–	criteria	9
clinch	–	console	–	croquet	–
clod	–	conspicuous	9	crossroad	–
cloves	–	constable	–	crucial	–
cobalt	–	Constantinople	–	crude	6
cock	–	consume	11	Cuba	5
collide	6	contaminate	7	cud	–
Colombia	–	contempt	–	cult	–
colonel	6	context	–	cunning	6
Columbia	9	contingent	–	curfew	–
coma	7	contour	7	currency	8
combustion	9	contraption	–	cutter	7
commission	9	contribute	5	czar	–
commit	6	convent	–	Czechoslovakia	–
compact	7	converse	7	dainty	–
compatible	–	convey	6	dale	–
compress	–	Copenhagen	–	Danube	–
comprise	–	cornerstone	–	daub	–
con	10	corps	9	Dayton	3
conceit	7	corporal	–	deacon	–
conceive	–	corpse	9	dean	4
concept	9	corrode	–	debate	5
concussion	–	corrupt	11	debris	–
condemn	7	cosmos	–	debut	–
conduct	12	countenance	–	decade	9
confederate	6	cowlick	–	deceive	7
confer	–	cramp	–	decode	7
confide	–	crankshaft	–	decor	–

decree	–	discreet	–	eccentric	7
deduct	–	discriminate	–	ecru	–
defect	9	disgust	7	ecstasy	–
deflect	–	dismay	5	Ecuador	9
deft	–	disrupt	6	eddy	–
defy	–	dissect	8	Edinburgh	–
deject	–	distort	–	eggplant	–
delegate	7	distract	10	ego	–
delinquent	11	district	6	eject	11
delirious	7	ditto	–	elaborate	5
denounce	–	ditty	–	elder	6
deplete	–	divine	–	elevate	6
derby	–	doctrine	–	eligible	7
dermis	6	doldrums	–	eliminate	7
derrick	5	domain	9	eloquent	7
despair	7	don	6	embark	9
despise	–	dormant	–	ember	–
despite	6	dormer	–	embryo	–
detach	7	dormitory	10	emotion	7
detail	7	dose	–	enamel	8
detain	–	dour	–	endure	7
deteriorate	–	douse	–	enforce	9
devastate	7	Dover	–	engage	6
devise	–	draftsperson	–	enigma	–
dialogue	7	drastic	7	ensemble	–
diction	11	dredge	–	enterprise	9
diesel	7	drone	6	entity	–
diligent	7	drudge	–	entrust	–
dilute	–	dub	–	enzyme	–
dinghy	–	Dublin	–	equilibrium	11
dingy	6	dunk	–	erect	7
diphtheria	–	duplicate	–	erode	8
diplomat	7	duration	12	escort	–
dire	–	dwell	–	estate	11
discard	9	dynamic	7	estuary	–
discharge	6	eavesdrop	–	etch	–

eternal	–	firefly	9	fuse	–
eucalyptus	8	fireproof	–	gadget	7
Eugene	7	fixture	9	gaggle	–
Euphrates	6	fjord	–	gait	9
evaluate	11	flagship	–	gallery	6
evergreen	6	flank	9	gamble	–
evident	7	flaunt	–	garb	7
evolve	–	fleet	10	garment	9
excavate	11	flinch	–	garnish	–
excerpt	7	floe	–	gash	–
exclude	–	florist	9	gaunt	–
execute	7	flounce	–	gauntlet	–
expand	7	flourish	6	gawky	–
exquisite	9	fluent	–	gene	7
external	9	flurry	–	generation	7
extract	7	foliage	9	genesis	–
extreme	6	fondle	–	genetic	7
eyesore	–	foresee	6	Geneva	–
Fairbanks	–	format	9	ghastly	7
fallow	7	fracture	6	ghoul	–
famine	7	fragile	7	Gibraltar	–
fanatic	9	frank	7	giddy	–
fantasy	7	fraught	–	gill	–
fatigue	6	frenzy	–	gimmick	9
feat	7	fright	–	gin	–
feeble	6	frigid	–	ginger	12
feldspar	–	frisk	–	gingerly	12
ferocious	7	fro	7	gladiator	–
fester	–	frogman	7	glean	–
fiancé		froth	–	glen	K
fickle	6	fugitive	9	glimmer	–
filament	12	fulfill	–	glint	–
fillet	–	fullback	7	glockenspiel	–
finance	7	fundamental	7	Gloucester	–
Finland	–	funeral	7	glower	–
firebox	4	furrow	–	glucose	7

gnat	–	harpsichord	10	hover	–
gneiss	–	hash	–	hub	–
goblet	–	haughty	9	huff	–
goo	4	Havana	7	Hungary	7
gorgeous	7	headlong	–	hurdle	8
gourd	6	headwaters	–	hurl	6
graft	6	headway	–	hustle	–
grant	7	Helena	11	hybrid	–
graphite	–	helm	–	hydraulic	–
greed	7	hemlock	6	hyena	–
Greenwich	–	hemoglobin	–	hygiene	–
gripe	–	hemp	–	hyperbole	–
grotesque	–	hence	7	hypnosis	–
grudge	9	herb	5	identical	6
gruel	–	heredity	7	idiom	–
grueling	–	heretofore	–	idol	–
Guam	–	hermit	7	igneous	5
guarantee	7	hideous	–	illuminate	–
guardian	6	hijack	–	immaculate	–
Guatemala	5	hilt	–	immense	6
Guiana	–	Himalayas	12	impact	9
guillotine	–	hinder	7	impair	7
guinea	8	Hiroshima	–	impertinent	–
gulch	–	hither	–	impose	12
hack	–	hitherto	–	imprint	3
hag	–	hoard	–	improvise	7
Haiti	5	Hollywood	6	incentive	11
hale	–	homer	7	incubate	–
halfback	–	homograph	–	indicate	6
hammerhead	6	homophone	–	indigo	–
handiwork	10	honeycomb	6	Indonesia	–
hanker	–	hospitality	–	induce	11
haphazard	11	host	7	inert	–
hardship	5	hostage	9	infer	–
Harlem	–	hothouse	–	inferno	–
harmony	7	hovel	–	influenza	–

infringe	–	jeer	6	leech	11
ingredient	7	jeopardy	–	legacy	–
inherit	–	jetliner	6	legible	10
initiate	–	jinx	–	legion	8
inject	–	jockey	7	legume	–
inoculate	–	jolt	–	Leipzig	–
instance	6	jounce	–	leisure	7
institute	8	jumble	–	levy	–
insulate	–	jury	6	liable	7
insure	7	jut	5	liberal	9
interfere	7	jute	–	lice	11
intern	–	Kenya	12	lichen	9
internal	7	keynote	–	lieutenant	11
interval	7	Kiev	4	ligament	–
intricate	12	Kilimanjaro	–	likewise	8
intrigue	–	kindle	11	limelight	–
invade	–	kink	–	limerick	7
invaluable	–	knapsack	6	lingerie	–
Iraq	12	knoll	11	linseed	–
Ireland	11	Korea	12	liquor	–
iridescent	–	krypton	–	listless	7
isolate	6	Labrador	12	livid	–
isthmus	–	lacquer	11	lodestone	–
italics	–	lagoon	9	logic	7
ivory	–	Lancaster	–	lore	–
ivy	8	lance	–	lubricate	–
jackal	–	landholder	–	lug	–
jade	–	landscape	5	lukewarm	–
jalopy	–	Laos	–	lull	–
Jamaica	5	lard	–	luminous	–
jamb	–	Laredo	–	lure	5
Jamestown	4	lasagna	8	lurk	–
jangle	–	laser	7	lush	9
Java	5	lateral	–	luster	–
javelin	9	lax	7	lute	–
jazz	6	Lebanon	12	Luxembourg	–

lyre	–	merge	6	moron	–
madam	7	meridian	7	morsel	–
mademoiselle	9	Mesopotamia	–	mortar	10
Madrid	5	metamorphosis	10	mortuary	–
magnesium	11	metaphor	10	mosaic	–
majority	7	metropolis	–	motive	7
makeshift	–	mica	6	muck	–
malaria	–	microbe	–	muddle	–
Malaysia	–	migrant	9	muffle	7
Manchester	3	mil	10	musket	–
Manchuria	–	Milan	6	mutton	–
mandolin	–	miller	11	mystify	–
mangle	–	mimeograph	–	mythology	7
Manhattan	–	mince	–	naive	9
mania	–	minimum	8	Nantucket	–
mantis	–	mint	5	nape	–
manuscript	–	mirth	–	Naples	–
marathon	9	misery	12	narcotic	–
marksman	–	mishap	5	natal	–
marvel	6	mistletoe	12	nausea	–
massacre	–	moat	–	neglect	7
massage	–	mobile	–	negotiate	–
massive	6	molar	–	nerve	7
mate	6	molest	–	Newcastle	–
matinee	7	Mongol	–	Newfoundland	–
mauve	–	Mongolia	–	nick	3
maximum	9	monk	–	nip	–
maze	11	monogram	–	nobleman	7
media	7	monopoly	6	noose	–
median	10	monsoon	–	norm	–
medieval	–	Monterrey	–	Normandy	–
Melbourne	7	Montreal	4	noteworthy	–
membrane	9	moor	–	Nottingham	–
memo	6	moral	7	notwithstanding	–
menace	7	morgue	–	novice	11
mere	–	Morocco	–	nuisance	6

nutmeg	–	parson	–	pledge	6
nutrient	9	particle	9	pluck	–
nymph	5	passion	–	plush	9
obstinate	–	patriarch	–	ply	11
obverse	–	peasant	6	pock	–
odor	5	peddle	–	polecat	–
offhand	–	pedestal	–	ponder	–
offspring	12	pedestrian	9	populate	–
onslaught	–	pedigree	–	pork	6
Ontario	5	pemmican	–	porter	–
opaque	6	pendant	9	portray	7
oral	K	perceive	11	pose	8
ordeal	11	perch	–	possess	6
ore	7	peril	–	potassium	–
organism	5	persecute	–	potent	–
Oslo	–	persist	12	potential	5
osmosis	–	persuade	6	Prague	–
outback	–	petite	–	prance	–
outboard	9	petition	7	predicament	–
outlandish	–	petrify	–	predict	6
outlying	11	petty	6	preen	–
outrage	–	pew	–	preface	7
outwit	–	phenomenon	8	premises	7
ovation	–	Philippines	8	preside	–
overrun	–	philosophy	7	presto	–
overseas	–	phosphorus	11	prevail	–
overtake	7	phylum	10	prim	–
pamper	–	pickpocket	–	probation	6
pang	–	pier	6	prod	–
pantomime	6	pinnacle	–	progress	7
par	–	pinpoint	–	prohibit	7
parabola	–	piston	–	prominent	7
paradise	–	pitfall	–	prompt	12
Paraguay	10	plankton	5	prone	11
pare	–	plantation	7	proportion	6
parsley	6	plea	7	propose	6

prose	12	redcap	–	Rhine	–
prosecute	–	redeem	–	rift	11
prospect	11	reef	8	rig	–
prosper	–	reel	5	rigor	7
prow	–	referee	7	riot	–
psalm	–	reform	–	rivet	–
puck	–	refrain	–	robust	–
pulp	–	refresh	8	rodent	–
purge	–	refugee	6	romance	12
puss	–	refund	7	rotor	–
putt	–	regime	–	Rotterdam	–
Pyrenees	7	regiment	6	rouse	–
quake	9	regulate	7	ruffian	–
quintet	–	rehabilitate	–	rummage	–
rabbi	–	reject	12	rumple	–
rack	–	relic	–	rupture	–
radioactive	9	remedy	7	russet	–
raffle	7	remorse	–	rut	–
Rainier	–	repeal	7	rye	9
ram	9	repent	11	sacrifice	6
ramble	–	repute	–	Salvador	–
random	9	request	7	sane	–
ransack	–	reside	7	Saskatchewan	–
ransom	10	resolve	6	Savannah	5
rant	1	respire	–	savor	–
rape	–	restrain	11	sawhorse	–
ratio	4	restrict	7	scald	–
rational	11	retail	6	scallop	–
rave	–	retain	7	scepter	–
ravel	–	retard	9	schooner	6
rawhide	–	retire	6	scope	–
react	–	retort	–	scoundrel	7
ream	–	retreat	–	scour	–
reciprocal	6	retrieve	–	scrag	–
reckon	–	revenge	6	scribe	–
recollect	–	revolve	6	scroll	–

scruff	–	sledge	–	squid	–
scurry	10	sleek	8	squire	–
scuttle	–	slither	–	standard	5
scythe	6	slouch	–	starling	–
seaway	–	sluice	–	statesman	7
sect	–	slur	–	stationary	10
sedan	9	smallpox	11	stature	6
seminary	–	smolder	–	stave	–
septic	–	smut	–	steed	–
sequence	6	snag	–	steeplechase	–
sequin	–	snuff	–	stein	5
serenade	7	socket	9	stellar	–
sergeant	7	solder	8	stench	–
serpent	9	solitude	6	stencil	–
serum	–	sophomore	–	steppe	–
shabby	7	soprano	–	stevedore	–
shackle	–	sorcery	–	stifle	–
shanty	–	soul	10	stigma	–
sheen	–	souse	–	Stockholm	–
sheer	11	spade	–	stout	11
shipshape	–	span	7	straddle	–
shoddy	–	Sparta	–	strand	9
shortcake	–	spawn	–	strongbox	–
shrine	7	specify	–	stronghold	7
shuttle	5	spectrum	5	stucco	–
Siberia	–	speculate	–	stupor	–
Sicily	–	spellbound	7	subdue	6
sickle	9	spew	–	sublime	–
siege	–	spindle	–	submit	7
silhouette	–	spinet	–	substitute	6
silo	–	spleen	–	subtle	9
simmer	–	splint	–	succulent	–
sine	–	splotch	–	sue	2
sinew	–	splurge	–	suffocate	–
sinister	5	spry	9	sullen	–
sizzle	–	squabble	12	sultry	–

summon	–	terminate	–	treacherous	–
sunspot	9	Thailand	12	tread	6
superintendent	–	therapy	9	treason	–
supervise	–	thermostat	–	trellis	–
supplement	9	thesaurus	6	tress	6
surge	8	thorough	9	trial	6
surplus	7	threshold	11	tribune	–
surrender	–	throne	12	trifle	–
suspend	9	throttle	–	trigonometry	–
suspense	–	thrust	6	trolley	–
swab	–	tiara	–	truant	–
swath	–	tier	–	tuberculosis	–
Sweden	6	titter	–	tungsten	–
swerve	12	toddle	–	turbine	9
swivel	–	toggle	–	turmoil	10
Sydney	10	token	–	turpentine	9
symphony	5	tolerate	10	tusk	6
synagogue	6	tonic	–	tutor	6
synthetic	6	topaz	–	twilight	–
Syria	–	topple	–	twinge	–
Tacoma	–	torment	–	typhoon	–
tailor	7	torrent	–	tyrant	5
talc	–	torture	7	uncanny	7
tallow	10	totter	–	underhanded	–
tally	8	tournament	9	unique	6
talon	–	towhead	–	unison	–
tangible	–	trait	9	urchin	12
tapestry	11	traitor	–	urn	11
tarnish	7	trance	–	utensil	11
taut	–	tranquil	–	utmost	6
taxidermy	–	transfer	2	utter	–
teak	–	transform	–	vagabond	–
technique	6	transfusion	–	vague	6
teller	7	transmit	8	valid	6
tenant	–	transparent	5	valise	–
tendon	–	travail	–	valor	–

valve	6	vise	–	whiskey	–
vaudeville	–	vocal	6	wholesale	6
velocity	8	volt	7	wholesome	6
vendor	9	vomit	–	wicket	–
veneer	–	vulgar	–	Williamsburg	7
venom	9	wafer	–	wilt	7
ventricle	12	wage	9	windfall	–
venture	9	Wales	–	windlass	–
verbal	9	wallop	–	wisecrack	–
verdict	7	warble	–	woe	–
version	7	ward	10	wombat	5
versus	–	warden	9	worthwhile	9
veteran	9	warfare	7	wrath	–
vice	9	Warsaw	12	wrench	7
vicinity	7	wary	11	wrought	–
vicious	5	watercress	–	wry	7
victor	6	waterlog	–	yam	–
Vienna	10	watershed	–	yearn	–
Vietnam	12	watt	7	yoga	–
vigil	–	welt	–	yule	–
villa	11	whereupon	–	zest	7
villain	–	whisk	–		

REFERENCES

Anderson, R. C., and Nagy, W. E. "The Vocabulary Conundrum." Urbana, Ill.: Center for the Study of Reading, Mar. 1993.

Anglin, J. M. *Vocabulary Development: A Morphological Analysis.* Monographs of the Society for Research in Child Development, 1993, *58*(10).

Baker, S. K., Simmons, D. C., and Kame'enui, E. J. *Vocabulary Acquisition: Synthesis of the Research.* Eugene, Ore.: National Center to Improve the Tools of Educators, 1995.

Baumann, J. F., and Kame'enui, E. J. "Research on Vocabulary Instruction: Ode to Voltaire." In J. Flood, J. J. Lapp, and J. R. Squire (eds.), *Handbook of Research on Teaching the English Language Arts.* Old Tappan, N.J.: Macmillan, 1991.

Baumann, J. F., Kame'enui, E. J., and Ash, G. E. "Research on Vocabulary Instruction: Voltaire Redux." In J. Flood, D. Lapp, J. R. Squire, and J. M. Jensen (eds.), *Handbook of Research on Teaching the English Language Arts.* (2nd ed.) Mahwah, N.J: Erlbaum, 2003.

Beck, I. L., and McKeown, M. G. "Conditions of Vocabulary Acquisition." In R. Barr, M. L. Kamil, P. Mosenthal, and P. D. Pearson (eds.), *Handbook of Reading Research.* White Plains, N.Y.: Longman, 1991.

Beck, I. L., McKeown, M. G., and Kucan, L. *Bringing Words to Life: Robust Vocabulary Instruction.* New York: Guilford Press, 2002.

Beck, I., McKeown, M., and Omanson, R. "The Effects and Uses of Diverse Vocabulary Instructional Techniques." In M. McKeown and M. Curtis (eds.), *The Nature of Vocabulary Acquisition.* Mahwah, N.J.: Erlbaum, 1987.

Becker, W. C., Dixon, R., and Anderson-Inman, L. *Morphographic and Root Word Analysis of 26,000 High Frequency Words.* Eugene: University of Oregon, College of Education, 1980.

Blachowicz, C.L.Z., and Fisher, P. "Vocabulary Instruction." In M. L. Kamil, P. B. Mosenthal, P. D. Pearson, and R. Barr (eds.), *Handbook of Reading Research.* Mahwah, N.J.: Erlbaum, 2000.

Bransford, J., Brown, A., and Cocking, R. (eds.). *How People Learn: Brain, Mind, Experience, and School.* (Exp. ed.) Washington, D.C: National Academy Press, 2000.

Burger, H. C. *The Wordtree.* Merriam, Kans.: Wordtree, 1984.

California Achievement Tests (Form E). Monterey, Calif.: CTB/McGraw-Hill, 1986.

Carroll, J., Davies, P., and Richman, B. *The American Heritage Word Frequency Book.* Boston: Houghton Mifflin, 1971.

Chall, J. S. *Readability: An Appraisal of Research and Application.* Columbus: Ohio State University, 1958.

Chall, J. S., Jacobs, V. A., and Baldwin, L. E. *The Reading Crisis: Why Poor Children Fall Behind.* Cambridge, Mass.: Harvard University Press, 1990.

Comprehensive Tests of Basic Skills (Form U). Monterey, Calif.: CTB/McGraw-Hill, 1984.

Cunningham, A. E., and Stanovich, K. E. "What Reading Does for the Mind." *American Educator,* 1998, *22*(1&2), 8–15.

Dupuy, H. P. *The Rationale, Development and Standardization of a Basic Word Vocabulary Test.* Washington, D.C.: Government Printing Office, 1974.

Frayer, D. A., Frederick, W. D., and Klausmeier, H. J. *A Schema for Testing the Level of Concept Mastery.* Madison: Wisconsin Research and Development Center for Cognitive Learning, 1969.

Gardner, E. F., Rudman, H. C., Karlsen, B., and Merwin, J. C. *Stanford Achievement Test* (Form E). Orlando, Fla.: Harcourt, 1981.

Graves, M. F. "Vocabulary Learning and Instruction." In E. Z. Rothkopf and L. C. Ehri (eds.), *Review of Research in Education.* Washington, D.C.: American Educational Research Association, 1986.

Graves, M. F., Brunetti, G. J., and Slater, W. H. "The Reading Vocabularies of Primary Grade Children of Varying Geographic and Social Backgrounds." In J. A. Niles and L. A. Harris (eds.), *New Inquiries in Reading Research and Instruction.* Rochester, N.Y.: National Reading Conference, 1982.

Hamilton, V. *The House of Dies Drear.* Old Tappan, N.J.: Macmillan, 1968.

Harris, A., and Jacobson, M. *Basic Elementary Reading Vocabularies.* Old Tappan, N.J.: Macmillan, 1972.

Harrison, C. *Readability in the Classroom.* Cambridge: Cambridge University Press, 1980.

Hirsch, D., and Nation, P. "What Vocabulary Size Is Needed to Read Unsimplified Texts for Pleasure?" *Reading in a Foreign Language,* 1992, *8*(2), 689–696.

Jenkins, J. R., Stein, M. L., and Wysocki, K. "Learning Vocabulary Through Reading." *American Educational Research Journal,* 1984, *2*(4), 767–787.

Johnson, D. D., and Pearson, P. D. *Teaching Reading Vocabulary.* (2nd ed.) New York: Holt, 1984.

Juster, N. *The Phantom Tollbooth*: New York: Random House, 1971.

Kurland, B. F., and Snow, C. E. "Longitudinal Measurement of Growth in Definitional Skill." *Journal of Child Language,* 1997, *24*(3), 603–625.

Lamott, A. *Bird by Bird: Some Instructions on Writing and Life.* New York: Pantheon, 1994.

Lazar, R. T., Warr-Leeper, G. A., Nicholson, C. B., and Johnson, S. "Elementary School Teachers' Use of Multiple Meaning Expressions." *Language, Speech, and Hearing Services in Schools,* 1989, *20,* 420–430.

Lesaux, N. K., and Siegel, L. S. "The Development of Reading in Children Who Speak English as a Second Language." *Developmental Psychology,* 2003, *39*(6), 1005–1019.

Levorato, M. C., and Cacciari, C. "The Effects of Different Tasks on the Comprehension and Production of Idioms in Children." *Journal of Experimental Child Psychology,* 1995, *60*(2), 261–283.

Lewin, R. A. *The Biology of Algae and Diverse Other Verses.* Pacific Grove, Calif.: Boxwood Press, 1997.

Marzano, R. J. *Building Background Knowledge for Academic Achievement: Research on What Works in Schools.* Alexandria, Va.: Association for Supervision and Curriculum Development, 2004.

Marzano, R. J., Kendall, J. S., and Paynter, D. E. *Analysis and Identification of Basic Words in Grades K–6.* Aurora, Colo.: Mid-Continent Research for Education and Learning, 1991.

Marzano, R. J., Pickering, D. J., and Pollock, J. E. *Classroom Instruction That Works: Research-Based Strategies for Increasing Student Achievement.* Alexandria, Va.: Association for Supervision and Curriculum Development, 2001.

Marzano, R. J., Norford, J. S., Paynter, D. E., Pickering, D. J., and Gaddy, B. B. *A Handbook for Classroom Instruction That Works.* Alexandria, Va.: Association for Supervision and Curriculum Development, 2001.

Nagy, W., and Anderson, R. "How Many Words Are There in Printed School English?" *Reading Research Quarterly,* 1984, *19*, 303–330.

Nagy, W. E., Herman, P., and Anderson, R. "Learning Word Meanings from Context During Normal Reading." *American Educational Research Journal,* 1987, *24*, 237–270.

National Reading Panel. *Teaching Children to Read: An Evidence-Based Assessment of the Scientific Research Literature on Reading and Its Implications for Reading Instruction.* Bethesda, Md.: National Institute of Child Health and Development, 2000.

Ogden, C. K. *The Basic Words: A Detailed Account of Uses.* London: Landor and Kegan Paul, 1932.

Read, J. *Assessing Vocabulary.* Cambridge: Cambridge University Press, 2000.

Ryder, R. J., and Graves, M. F. "Vocabulary Instruction Presented Prior to Reading in Two Basal Readers." *Elementary School Journal,* 1994, *95*, 139–153.

Schank, R. C., and Rieger, C. J. "Inference and the Computer Understanding of Natural Language." *Artificial Intelligence,* 1974, *5*, 373–412.

Schwartz, R. "Learning to Learn Vocabulary in Content Area Textbooks." *Journal of Reading,* 1988, *32*(2), 108–118.

Science Research Associates Survey of Basic Skills Objectives (Form P). Chicago: Science Research Associates, 1984.

Snow, C. E., Burns, S. M., and Griffin, P. (eds.). *Preventing Reading Difficulties in Young Children.* Washington, D.C.: National Academy Press, 1998.

Stahl, S. A. "Four Questions About Vocabulary Knowledge and Reading and Some Answers." In C. Hynd (ed.), *Learning from Text Across Conceptual Domains.* Mahwah, N.J.: Erlbaum, 1998.

Stahl, S. A., and Fairbanks, M. M. "The Effects of Vocabulary Instruction: A Model-Based Meta-Analysis." *Review of Educational Research,* 1986, *56,* 72–110.

Sticht, T. G., Hofstetter, R. C., and Hofstetter, C. H. "Knowledge, Literacy, and Power." *Communication Research,* 1997, *26*(1), 58–80. [http://www.coreknowledge.org/CKproto2/about/eval/KnowledgeLitandPower.htm].

Suhor, C. "Toward a Semiotics-Based Curriculum." *Journal of Curriculum Studies,* 1984, *16,* 247–257.

Thorndike, R. L., and Lorge, I. *The Teacher's Word Book of 30,000 Words.* New York: Teachers College Press, 1943.

Underwood, B. J. "Attributes of Memory." *Psychological Review,* 1969, *76,* 559–573.

Venezky, R. L. *The American Way of Spelling: The Structure and Origins of American English Orthography.* New York: Guilford Press, 1999.

Watts, S. M. "Vocabulary Instruction During Reading Lessons in Six Classrooms." *Journal of Reading Behavior,* 1995, *27,* 339–424.

Wood, K. E. "Using Story Grammar to Improve Students' Reading and Writing Abilities." *The Reading Teacher,* Feb. 1984, pp. 496–499.

INDEX

Burger, H. C., 128
Burns, S. M., 7

C

Cacciari, C., 18
California Achievement Tests (CAT), 130, 133
Cardinal numbers, 132–133
Carroll, J., 128–129, 132, 135
Chall, J. S., 7, 18
Choosing the right word, sample sentences for, 75
Classroom practices, aligning with standards/benchmarks, 85
Cluster Beanbag (game), 64
Cluster walls. *See* Semantic cluster walls
Cocking, R., 4
Cognates, and ELL students, 19
Colorful Songs (game), 64
Commercial vocabulary programs, 122
Complex vocabulary: introducing, 76; requirement of, 35
Compound words, 15
Comprehensive Tests of Basic Skills (CTBS), 106, 130, 133
Concept definition maps, 51
Conceptual knowledge, and robust vocabulary, 4
Connotations, 16
Constructed responses, 110
Content-area vocabulary, 17, 26
Context: and encounters with new words, 26; and upper elementary students, 18

Contractions, 16
Conventional quizzes, 108–110
Cunningham, A. E., 17
Customized word list, 122; assesment-related words, 87; basic words, 86; categorizing words on, 97–99; creating, 81; fiction/nonfiction sources, 87; form for recording words for, 89; language arts experiences, vocabulary from, 92–93; national/state/district assessments, vocabulary from, 93; need for, 83; resources for creating, 83–87; standards-based lists, adding basic words to, 90–91; standards-based vocabulary, identifying, 88–90; state/district standards/benchmarks documents, 84–85; steps in creating, 88–93

D

Davies, P., 128–129, 132, 135
Denotations, 16
Descriptive pattern graphic organizers, 50
Dictionary, and word meanings, 41–44
Direct instruction, 30–31, 33; categorizing words for, 98–99; framework/strategies for, 35–68; goals of, 30; scheduling experiences, 100–103; steps for learning new words, 36–55; student generation of explanations, 38–45; teacher explanation of new word's meaning, 37–38; teacher identification of

new word/eliciting of background knowledge, 37; visual representations of students, 45–55

"Disaster Dictionary," 73

District assessments, vocabulary from, 93

District standards/benchmarks, 84–85

Dixon, R., 127, 128, 130

Dull paragraph, and revisions, example of, 28

Dupuy, H. P., 128

E

Electronic sources, and word meanings, 45

English Language Learners (ELL), 18–19; and cognates, 19; and effective vocabulary programs, 22

Essential word list

Evyindsson, H., 100

Expanded vocabularies: fourth through sixth grades, 17–18; kindergarten through first grade, 13–14; second and third grades, 15–16; second language learners, 19

F

Fairbanks, M. M., x

Feminine forms of nouns, 131

Field trip follow-up, 71

Figurative language: and primary-grade students, 14; and second and third graders, 16; and upper elementary students, 18

Fisher, P., x

Foreign words, 131

Formal definition skills, and upper elementary students, 18

Fourth through sixth grades: expanded vocabularies, 17–18; metalinguistic awareness, 17; typical word knowledge, 17; vocabulary strategies, 17–18

Frayer, D. A., 51

Frayer model, 51, 53–54, 110

Frederick, W. D., 51

G

Games/word play, 63–68. *See also* Word games

Gardner, J., 48

Grade-level designations, intercorrelation between (table), 135

Graphic organizers, 50–51

Graphic representations, for learning new words, 38–39

Graves, M. F., 7, 103

Griffin, P., 7

Group activities, using for performance assessments, 111

H

Harris, A., 129, 130

Harrison, C., 7

Herman, P., x

Hirsch, D., 17

Hofstetter, C. H., 7

Hofstetter, R. C., 7

Homophones, 63

House of Dies Drear, The (Hamilton), 75

I

Idiomatic language, 16; and second language learners, 19

Idioms, 63

Incidental learning: books/resources to enhance vocabulary learning, selecting, 73–76; planning for, 69–80; read-aloud experiences, selecting, 80; students' wide reading experiences, expanding, 78–80; vocabulary-rich environment, creating, 69–76

Incidental learning experiences, 33; planned, 32; planning for, 31–32; random, 31–32

Inflected forms, 131

Internet, and word meanings, 45

Iowa Test of Basic Skills, 106

J

Jacobs, V. A., 18

Jacobson, M., 129, 130

Jenkins, J. R., 25

Jesse, D., 127*fn*

Johnson, S., 21

Jokes, 16

Juster, N., 11

K

Kame'enui, E. J., x, 103

Kendall, J. S., xiv, 127

Kindergarten through first grade: expanded vocabularies, 13–14; meta-linguistic awareness, 13; typical word knowledge, 12–13; vocabulary learning, 12–14; vocabulary strategies, 14

Kinesthetic representations, 51–53

Klausmeier, H. J., 51

Kucan, L., 3

Kurland, B. F., 18

L

Labels, 3–4, 70–71; hearing, 4

Lamott, A., 125

Language arts experiences, vocabulary from, 92–93

Language awareness, and primary-grade students, 14

Lazar, R. T., 21

Lesaux, N. K., 19

Levorato, M. C., 18

Lewin, R. A., 13

Limited vocabularies, and early reading ability, 7

Listening vocabulary: fourth through sixth grades, 17; second and third grades, 15

Literal meanings, 16; and upper elementary students, 18

Looking up words, 72

Lorge, I., 128, 129

M

Marzano, R. J., xiv, 7, 22, 26, 78, 127

Masculine forms, of nouns, 131

Master of disguises, 75–76

Match Me (game), 64

McKeown, M., 3, 103, 129, 132, 136

"Meet-and-greet" new vocabulary words, 72–73

Mental pictures, generating, 47–49

Meta-linguistic awareness: fourth through sixth grades, 17; kindergarten through first grade, 13

Q

Questions, and word meanings, 40–43

Quizzes, 108–110

R

Random incidental learning experiences, 31–32

Read-aloud experiences, 15; selecting, 80

Reading, using for performance assessments, 111

Reading references, 121

Reading vocabulary: fourth through sixth grades, 17; second and third grades, 15

Reasonable resources, 73–74

Receptive vocabulary, 108

Red herring concept, 70–71

Richman, B., 128–129, 132, 135

Riddles, 63

Rieger, C. J., 127

Robust vocabulary: defined, 3; importance of, 1–10; learners with, 4; need for, 5–6; using with children, 74–76

Ryder, R. J., 7

S

Schank, R. C., 127

Schwartz, R., 51

Science Research Associates (SRA), 130, 133

Second and third grades, 15–17; expanded vocabularies, 15–16; meta-linguistic awareness, 16; and multiple word meanings, 16; typical word knowledge, 15; vocabulary strategies, 16–17

Second language learners, 19–20; expanded vocabularies, 19; typical word knowledge, 19; vocabulary strategies, 20

Self-assessment rubrics, 113–114

Semantic cluster walls, 76–78, 96; of careers and occupations, 77; for math vocabulary (sample), 79; purpose of, 77–78; as records of increased vocabulary learning, 78

Semantic feature analysis: completing, 61–62; student worksheet for, 62

Sentence stems, and word meanings, 40–41

Siegel, L. S., 19

Sight-recognition words, 86

Slater, W. H., 7

Slogans, 63

Snow, C. E., 7, 18

Stahl, S. A., x

Standardized tests, and vocabulary assessment, 122

Standards-based lists, adding basic words to, 90–91

Standards-based vocabulary, identifying, 88–90

Stanford Achievement Test, 130, 133

Stanovich, K. E., 17

State assessments, vocabulary from, 93

State standards/benchmarks, 84–85

Stein, M. L., 25

Sticht, T. G., 7

Students: discussions/conferences, 111–112; logs, 120–121; progress, assessing, 105–123

Suffixes, 15

Vocabulary instruction, planning, 8–10

Vocabulary learning: developmental aspects of, 11–22; fourth through sixth grades, 17–18; kindergarten through first grade, 12–14; modeling strategies for, 31; second and third grades, 15–17; second language learners, 19–20; selecting books/resources to enhance, 73–76; steps for learning new words, 56–68; students deepen their understanding through, 56–63; students engage in vocabulary games/word play, 63–68; steps in, 117

Vocabulary Learning in My Classroom (self-reflection questionnaire), 9–10

Vocabulary notebooks, 116–120

Vocabulary predictions, 29–30

Vocabulary preview, 71

Vocabulary program, 20–22

Vocabulary Scramble (game), 66–67

Vocabulary size: and early reading ability, 7; and socioeconomic status (SES), 7

Vocabulary strategies: fourth through sixth grades, 17–18; kindergarten through first grade, 14; second and third grades, 16–17; second language learners, 20

Vocabulary teaching: direct instruction, planning for, 30–31; incidental learning experiences, planning for, 31–32; multiple learning experiences, offering, 25–26; understanding approaches to, 23–33

Vocabulary tests, 108–110

Vocabulary-rich environment, creating, 69–76

W

Warr-Leeper, G. A., 21

Watts, S. M., 7

Weekly tests, 108–110

Wittgenstein, L., 1

Word attack skills, 16–17

Word consciousness, 4

Word detective, 70–71

Word games, 63–68; Cluster Beanbag, 64; Colorful Songs, 64; Match Me, 64; Pass the Right Word, 66; Pyramid Clusters, 67–68; Vocabulary Bingo, 64–65; Vocabulary Scramble, 66–67

Word knowledge: fourth through sixth grades, 17; kindergarten through first grade, 12–13; second and third grades, 15; second language learners, 19

Word meanings: and dictionary, 41–44; and electronic sources, 45; and Internet, 45; multiple, 14, 16, 21; and questions, 40–43; and sentence stems, 40–41; and thesaurus, 44

Word play, 16